P9-DIB-143

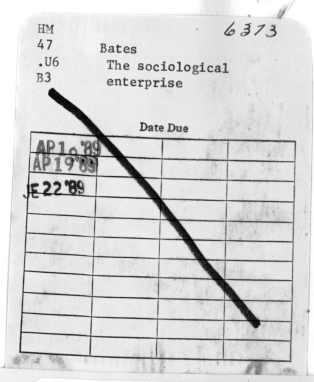

Under the editorship of
Ernest Q. Campbell

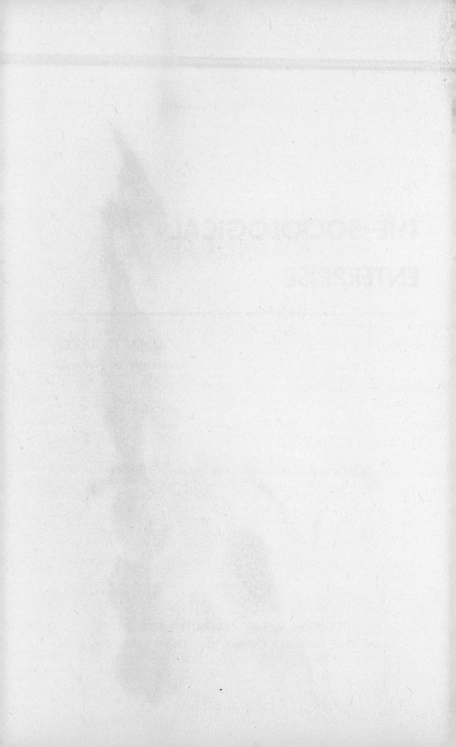

THE SOCIOLOGICAL ENTERPRISE

ALAN P. BATES
University of Nebraska

HOUGHTON MIFFLIN COMPANY · BOSTON
New York · Atlanta · Geneva, ILL. · Dallas · Palo Alto

Sociology is among the most exciting disciplines in contemporary American education. Its growth in the last two decades, whether indexed in terms of student appeal, numbers entering the field professionally, scholarly productivity, recognition of its relevance by cognate disciplines, or the sheer growth in quality of its concerns and modes of inquiry, has been most impressive. More important, there is every indication that this growth will continue and probably accelerate. There are several important reasons for this. For one, the preoccupying debates over how quantitative the data should be, whether sociology is, can, or should be scientific, and over whether empirical research can be worthwhile if it is not directly tied to important theoretical concerns—these debates, which were necessary for a young discipline but which also consumed a good bit of its energy, are now largely matters of the past. Another reason is the nation's continuing and increasing concern with social reform which requires that we know more about the lives of our citizens, what they need, how they live, why they respond as they do. Yet another reason is a growing comparative perspective across nations, which in the broadest sense is concerned with how widely human institutions, values, and typical responses vary across time and space. And finally, the range of settings in which the sociologist applies his skills is expanding to government, industry, research institutes, and private foundations, to complement his work in the traditional halls of ivy; and even within these college and university confines, the sociologist is found increasingly in schools of law, medicine, theology, business, and journalism as well as the traditional arts and sciences setting.

Students and those who advise them deserve to know what the

professional enterprise called sociology is all about; if they do not, they will either miss an excellent intellectual and occupational opportunity altogether, or they may enter it less well informed than they ought to be. Professor Alan Bates has written *The Sociological Enterprise* as one protection against such pitfalls. It is an honest, careful attempt to describe the intellectual perspective, the problem-sense, and the work styles of sociologists, as well as the organization of the discipline. It will be immensely useful to beginning students who want a bird's-eye view, but no less useful to entering graduate students who will profit from the book's perspective and balance. Advisors and guidance counsellors in college and high school will find it readable and informative. Professor Bates writes lucidly and with a sensitive understanding of the profession he practices. He communicates his obvious fascination with the problems the sociologist tackles and the way he goes about extending the range of human knowledge. Students just being introduced to the discipline will want to continue the journey after reading this book, and those already committed to its study will gain a clearer insight into how its various parts hang together. From among its readers will come that growing number who major in sociology and continue graduate study in it, and that is all to the nation's good.

ERNEST Q. CAMPBELL

Vanderbilt University

This book has two objectives. First, it attempts to characterize sociology as a disciplinary field, communicating something of the sociologist's intellectual orientation toward behavior and defining his subject matter in general terms. Second, it presents considerable information on sociology as a profession within which some student readers might some day find a personal career.

Both topics are discussed in greater detail than is available in introductory texts or in texts concerned with more specialized subjects in sociology. Both, it seems to me, are important to undergraduate pedagogy in this field. The general viewpoint of the sociologist, once acquired, is perhaps the most useful single thing a student can hope to gain from his contact with the discipline, whether he is developing a long-run interest or is simply including sociology in a general education program. Some knowledge of sociological training, careers, and the social organization of the profession are sharply relevant to sociology's staffing needs in a time of rapid expansion and competition with related disciplines for competent young people.

The technical language of sociology is almost completely absent here. Yet, while the book should be easily understood by college underclassmen, it contains information not known to most beginning graduate students. Hence, it may be useful collateral reading in the beginning course and in the first year of graduate training as well as in the more advanced, summarizing courses sometimes taken by sociology majors in the senior year.

ALAN P. BATES

Lincoln, Nebraska

CONTENTS

THE SOCIOLOGICAL ENTERPRISE

I

THE SOCIOLOGICAL
VIEW OF HUMAN
BEHAVIOR

This chapter has a single objective: to introduce the sociological view of human behavior. The reader may be enrolled in a first course in sociology or may even have begun graduate training, but the chances are that in neither case has a genuine sociological outlook yet been acquired. The completion of any given number of courses in the field (even with high grades) no more guarantees the special kind of learning under discussion than the completion of four years in a liberal arts college guarantees that a person is well educated.

The sociological perspective is initially not easy to grasp. Nevertheless, the considerable effort needed is worth exerting, because, once mastered, a valuable, permanent addition to one's resources for understanding and coping with experience is gained. A short discussion of why there are some difficulties here will introduce our topic.

MODELS FOR UNDERSTANDING
BEHAVIOR

The term "model" may be applied to fairly inclusive pictures we acquire of what the world is like and what orientations toward it are appropriate. In the normal course of events each of us acquires a number of models of the experienced world. For any one of us, society is the main source of these world views. We do not invent them ourselves, although each individual version differs slightly from any other. They come to us little by little, from our parents, the activities of childhood play groups, the adult lives going on around us as we grow up, from books, television, school, and many other places. Our own physical and psychological characteristics interact with the incoming models as the years go by. Slowly the pictures of what the world is (and ought to be) take form in our developing minds.

From the human point of view the world is infinitely various and many models of what it is like are possible. The process of acquiring new points of view about experience need not end at any particular point in an individual's life cycle. It is possible at any age to acquire a new way of looking at familiar things and hence to discover, as it were, a new world. Perhaps part of what we mean by continued growth in adult life is the ability to acquire new perspectives.

The sociological model of human behavior is not inherently more difficult to grasp than are others, yet in practice problems are often encountered. This is so primarily because more familiar perspectives interfere. Everyone has extensive informal and sometimes formal training in several of these more familiar perspectives. For example, nearly everyone has a good deal of general knowledge these days about the structure and functioning of the human body and how physiological factors may influence behavior. Each of us uses a biological model to help us understand some of our experience.

We are equally accustomed to thinking about behavior in psychological terms. Words like "mind," "personality," and "motive" are signposts that direct us toward the individual's psychological organization as a source of conduct. "My friend behaves that way because he has an introverted personality," we say, and curiosity as to what lies back of the friend's actions is satisfied. Psychological models of behavior are exceedingly popular today. Moral perspectives on experience are just as well known. Here, behavior is perceived and related to by comparing it to standards of right and wrong, good and evil. "He is a good man," one says, or "You had no right to do that." When one talks this way he expects to be understood even if not always agreed with.

Sometimes deliberately, sometimes quite unthinkingly, people use one or another of such models to help them come to terms with virtually every experience in life. Through them each person can draw on the accumulated knowledge and wisdom of the human species. In their broadest forms each perspective is available to all, even though each is also the subject of highly specialized study. One need not be a professional psychologist to think about life in essentially psychological terms.

But people do not often think about experience in sociological terms. Sociology came late in the intellectual history of mankind and its specialized approach to understanding behavior has not yet become common knowledge, even among the educated. One does not grow up absorbing its essential point of view as one does with older models. As a consequence, when a person first meets sociology, as in an introductory course, the tendency is to fit the contents of the field into nonsociological perspectives already known. This is not done deliberately, of course, but the result is that sociology's most important contribution to understanding is lost.

To the social aspects of human experience sociology brings a unique and valid perspective unlike any other. It is not a better perspective than those provided by alternative models; it is different. Each of the major models which have evolved over time address themselves to some, but never all of the facets of that complex creature, man. Each is especially appropriate in some situations, but not in all circumstances. Both these statements are true of sociology too. Each perspective looks at the human scene and abstracts from the whole those features to which it is particularly sensitive. No model is sensitive to all the ways in which human behavior may be perceived as significant and orderly. Sociology, in taking its place alongside older perspectives, adds a new dimension to man's understanding of man without supplanting older orientations.

To visualize these points in a simple setting, consider a family group which has just finished its evening meal and is sitting around the table discussing the day's events. As the participants live through this scene it is all of a piece, a unitary thing — just a typical meal in a family setting. But if one stands back a bit, becomes an onlooker, and seeks to "understand" the behavior taking place, alternative viewpoints are possible. A physiologist might say, "They have just eaten, so bodily tension has been relieved, equilibrium restored, and a general feeling of well being has resulted." A psychologist might watch for a while, then say, "Well, it's clear that learning is taking place. Notice how the parents frowned when the little boy told them he had made an impudent reply to one of his teachers, then smiled approvingly when he hastened to say that he had apologized for his remark. The parents are trying to reinforce some kinds of behavior and extinguish others." A minister looks on for a while, then observes that this is a nice family. "They're good parents," he says. "You can tell that they want the kids to learn the difference between right and wrong, and I notice they talk about attending church too." A sociological observer might watch and perhaps say: "Here is an upper-middle class family with a marked equalitarian authority pattern. The oldest girl is beginning to feel a strong conflict of loyalty between her parents and her peer group."

Each onlooker pays particular attention to some aspects of this incident and ignores or pays less attention to others. Each viewpoint has something to contribute to our understanding of the whole. The value of any one point of view depends mostly upon the nature of the problem considered at the moment. A really well educated person knows several models of human behavior, and — equally important — is a good judge of which model is most appropriate for a given set of circumstances. There are many situations involving social behavior in which sociology's orientation is most helpful. Unfortunately, because it is comparatively unknown, other models are often misfitted to situations which call for the sociologist's special viewpoint.

SOCIOLOGY'S PERSPECTIVE

Sociology overlaps its sister fields in many ways, but, like each of them, it has a distinctive orientation toward its subject matter.

Most broadly and fundamentally, it is concerned with how human social behavior is organized and how this organization changes over time. Just now these words may convey little meaning, or may have a deceptive simplicity, but they state the case for what is unique in the point of view of sociology. The key words in this statement are "social behavior," "organization," and "change."

Social Behavior

As a specialist, the sociologist is not interested in all behavior which affects and is affected by other people, only in that which is interpersonally relevant. Social behavior, a very inclusive notion, refers to all behavior meeting this criterion. Quite a few specialists are interested in social behavior, so we must push further in order to grasp the sociologist's particular concern. We come close to the heart of the matter by stating that the sociologist is chiefly interested in being able to make *general* statements about social behavior — that under such-and-such circumstances a given kind of behavior is likely to occur. Inkeles puts it well in saying that the primary concern of the sociologist is "in the study of those aspects of social life which are present in all social forms." [1]

Such a statement means that the sociologist is interested in such things as the organization of American cities, the way in which power is distributed in groups, the relationship between masculine and feminine roles, the factors which produce conforming and deviating behavior, the ways in which change is induced or resisted (not to mention many other problems, of course). By the same token he is not, as a specialist, concerned with the Boston Tea Party, the Wagner Labor Relations Act, the family life of the American president, a quarrel between two young lovers of his acquaintance, or the personality of his mother-in-law.

We must be as clear as possible about this. In its purest form the sociological frame of reference does not take into account the idiosyncrasies of single persons or of separate historical occurrences. Or, looking at an individual case from this perspective, it will be seen as a single instance of a more general class of similar instances, deviating to a greater or lesser extent from the characteristics of the class. In other words, sociology is or aspires to be a

[1] A. Inkeles, *What Is Sociology?* Foundations of Modern Sociology Series. Englewood Cliffs, N.J.: Prentice-Hall, 1964, p. 16.

generalizing science. In this it is like many other sciences. Human physiology is not the physiology of a single organism but of a class of organisms, and the characteristics of the class do not precisely describe all the attributes of a single case. As a science psychology is not concerned with the behavior of one particular human, but with that of classes of humans *seen as individuals*. The sociologist also is interested in the behavior of people, but only that behavior which links people together, at a level at which he can generalize about classes of such behavior.

Here is an example of a sociological generalization: "In American cities there is an inverse relation between the incidence of reported crime and distance from the center of the city." Note that there is no reference to any particular city, no mention of which persons actually commit crimes, or what kinds of personalities they have, only a statement of the relation between a condition and a class of social behavior. Here is another. "The higher the rank of a person within a group, the more nearly his activities conform to the norms of the group." [2] Again, no particular group is mentioned, the nature of the norms is not specified, and the many differences among group members are ignored.

When one first encounters the sociological perspective and begins to grasp its nature, an initial reaction may be that it omits one of the most important things about human behavior: that which is unique in each occurrence and in each person. Actually, the sociologist does not mean to belittle in any way such elements in human experience. In his personal life he is as sensitive to them as is anyone else. He does argue that there is a level of human behavioral organization, the social level, which is of enormous importance, and about which it is possible to develop a generalizing science which deliberately ignores the individual case in order to be able to discover how human behavior is socially organized.

Social Organization

The sociologist is interested in organized social behavior. Put very generally, this means that behavior which links together in-

---

[2] G. C. Homans, *The Human Group*. New York: Harcourt, Brace, 1950, p. 141. This is Homans' famous "rank-conformity" hypothesis, which stimulated much research and discussion subsequent to its publication.

dividuals or groups of individuals is not random or haphazard. It has the properties of orderliness, pattern, repetitiveness, hence predictability. Here is a college classroom. During a particular semester at nine o'clock each morning, Monday through Friday, the room is filled with college students. Each goes without hesitation to a certain chair. A minute or two later a professor enters, stands at the front of the classroom, facing the students, and begins to talk. Most of the students write in notebooks. A few whisper covertly to one another. At the end of fifty minutes a bell rings, the professor ends his comments, the students close their notebooks, and all leave the room. We have here an identification and short description of an instance of *social* organization even though it does not use the technical language of sociology. It is clear that the behavior of these persons with respect to each other is patterned. This is true even though there are minor variations in the specific sequence of actions from one class meeting to the next. Our example includes no information about the psychological characteristics of students or teacher; it does not even mention the nature of the course, or whether it is advanced or elementary. We recognize a single specimen of a large class of social situations having a familiar kind of social organization which, by the way, significantly channels a good deal of human activity.

It is the *pattern of interdependent behavior* which interests the sociologist. This is the kind of unit he studies, not the individuals who participate in the pattern. He knows perfectly well that there are important differences between the class members and that from the viewpoint of another model, say, the psychological, these differences would be of first importance. But not for the sociologist. What is crucial for him is that all these persons, *despite their differences*, behave with respect to each other in an orderly, predictable fashion. Furthermore, he is not at all surprised to find that the patterned behavior of the people in this class closely resembles that of innumerable other classes, each with its own set of "unique" personalities and other special characteristics. Without knowing anything of the attributes of individuals in a given class he can know a good deal about how people will behave in this category of situations precisely because such settings are socially organized. True, he can't say a great deal about the psychological organization of individual students from knowledge of this kind of social organization. But by the same token, we cannot learn much about the social structure of college classrooms from the summated personality characteristics of college students. These are simply different levels of behavioral organization, interdependent to be sure, but not the same.

The order the sociologist sees in the social life of men is not perfect. Evidence of organization is sought in the pattern and predictability of actual behavior, but it is always true that some of the behavior in every situation does not fit the pattern and conform to the prediction. Similarly, if organization is described in cultural terms, it will be found that there is seldom, perhaps never complete agreement among all the actors on what behavior is called for in a particular real-life drama. There may even be radical disagreement on the cultural prescriptions. On the other hand, the fact that a group exists at all testifies that it is to some degree socially organized. Social organization is a "more or less" matter, and the sociologist is interested in differences in the degree of organization and the consequences for understanding behavior.

Social Change

The general statement about the sociological outlook made a few pages back indicated that this orientation is concerned not only with stability in social life but also with change. Consider the college classroom illustration again. It is possible to describe this situation as though there were no time dimension, and the sociologist often does this when he is primarily concerned with revealing the "structural" characteristics of a social situation. So we say that the classroom is organized so that the students sit in orderly rows facing the front of the room, each student occupying a particular spot in the arrangement. The instructor faces them, standing at the front. Interaction flows between the students and the instructor for the most part, with little student-student communication; students show more deference to the teacher than vice versa; and so on.

Such a description has a static quality. The fact is that what we see as social organization only becomes manifest with the passage of time, as was better suggested in our first reference to the classroom. First this event takes place, then that. We say there is organization and structure because the *sequence* of events is repetitive and predictable. The next session of the class will correspond closely to this one. Paradoxically, one form of change is a kind of absence of change. Since the pattern of events repeats itself over and over, we can observe change only as we watch the unfolding of a single manifestation of a pattern which itself does not alter.

A more familiar notion of change as applied to social organization involves some alteration in the patterned character of social behavior. The *pattern* is different, and presumably will not return to its former state. In a strict sense even very stable social organizations always undergo at least minor alterations through time. Our hypothetical college class will not have quite the same social organization ten weeks after its first session even though the main features of the structure appear to be the same. Similarly, on a larger scale, college classes in general are conducted somewhat differently today than their "sociological ancestors" were two or three generations ago.

Sociologists are interested in both cross-sectional, structural approaches to social phenomena and in time-dimensional, change approaches. Neither is inherently more important than the other. Both present fundamental problems to the discipline. The stability of social life and the inevitable accompanying change are taken for granted by laymen, but to sociologists they are a Janus-faced mystery that forever challenges.

THE SCOPE OF
SOCIOLOGICAL INTEREST

The sociologists's interest in the general characteristics of all social behavior can take him into the study of any particular manifestation: economic, political, religious, educational, aesthetic, or any other. Also, for him the entire social world is subdivisible into innumerable progressively smaller units. For instance, the United States constitutes for him a single social structure, so incredibly complex that the social sciences cannot very adequately describe it at their present stage of development. Included within this single structure are a number of major social institutions, each a smaller social world within the larger. Below the institutional level are hundreds of thousands of organizations and associations of varying size and complexity. Still lower down the scale of size and complexity are millions upon millions of small, relatively informal, and transient face-to-face groups, each containing subgroups. Finally, there are, in astronomically large numbers, single social acts, which can, if desired, be abstracted from context for analysis.

As a discipline sociology is interested in this whole range of social organization, as manifested in every sector of society and at every level of size and complexity. Furthermore, it is concerned with the interdependence of organization among different sectors and levels. In physical science man is interested in the features of the planet earth, but recognizes that part of his understanding of earth depends upon recognition that it is part of the solar system. Hence, the solar system is a level of organization of matter and energy worth studying too. But the solar system is part of a still larger organization known as a galaxy, and the galaxy of which our solar system is a part is only one among incredibly large numbers of other galaxies, all of which respond to some larger order of organization. In the social life of man, too, there are worlds within worlds, and while there is a rough inverse relation between size and complexity, the sociologist has learned to have a most healthy respect for the complexity of even the smallest and seemingly most simple unit of social organization.

It is worth stressing that sociology is concerned with all forms of organized social behavior. One sociologist, to be sure, may be interested only in the study of large, formal organizations, another in the structure of communities, a third in family disorganization. Specialization is as inevitable here as in other fields of knowledge. But the general viewpoint of sociology excludes no arena in which organized social behavior is found, and by the same token, the general viewpoint of the discipline will inform the specialized research of any true sociologist. This means that the importance or visibility of a phenomenon as a layman would see it is no criterion of its sociological interest. The discipline is interested in events where decisions of huge importance are weighed, but just as interested in homely, seemingly trivial, and commonplace events of everyday life. It is committed to the study of behavior that society judges deviant, bizarre, "bad," such as crime, alcoholism, and far-out religious cults, but no more so than to the analysis of conforming, normal, "good" behavior.

Culture

When the sociologist looks at his subject matter he makes a distinction between the social organization of people's actual conduct and the organization of people's ideas of what that behavior should be. This relationship is of utmost importance to him. A great deal of what social scientists call "culture" is made up of widely diffused ideas which either bear directly on social behavior or have indirect implications for actual behavior. While sometimes made a matter of written record, these ideas are crucially located in the minds of living people. It is not necessary to introduce the culture concept to readers of this book, but it is important in thinking about the sociological perspective to gain a general idea of how scholars in this discipline relate culture to actual conduct.

An analogy with helpful possibilities for our problem utilizes the drama. Culture is like the script of a play. Actors in a conventional play memorize the script before they go out onto the stage. Their performance each time the play is given may vary slightly from all previous performances. Nevertheless, what they do before their audience is always closely related to the script. In life, as we play out our parts in groups and organizations each of us performs according to a pre-existing script.

As analogies go this one isn't bad. It sets us thinking in the right direction, although like all analogies it is potentially misleading. For instance, there is the question of authorship. No single dramatist wrote the script of culture. It evolved through thousands of years, written by millions of persons, constantly undergoing modification and, in some respects, growth. Another difference lies in the attitude of the actor toward the play. Some actors, it is said, can temporarily immerse themselves completely in their parts, but by and large we may be sure that actors *know they are acting.* Most of the time in everyday life we are not aware of the degree to which social behavior is guided along the lines dictated by culture. Others besides sociologists and anthropologists, of course, sometimes achieve insights into this state of affairs, but such awareness is an essential part of the sociological perspective.

The analogy is imperfect in other respects too. Most plays (omitting some experimental variations in the contemporary theater) do not allow a great deal of latitude to the actor, at least insofar as speech is concerned. Variations in actual performance are likely to reflect the actor's skill in recreating the dramatist's intentions without departing from his written directions. But culture is not so restrictive on the ordinary actions of men. The script may occasionally be quite precise (the traditions for the inauguration of the American president), but more typically it gives only general instructions to the actors on the real life stage. Plenty of room is left for innovations, intended or inadvertent.

Finally, dramas in the conventional theater do not evolve out of the experience of the actors, whereas culture does. To the sociologist there is a complex interdependence between culture and social action. From one point of view, he seeks in culture some of the most important causes of human behavior. At the same time he also regards culture as a product or outcome of social behavior. In other words, even as the actors play out their parts according to the plan of the script they are by their very performance changing the script. In order to grasp the point it may be helpful to try to imagine a human group in which the social behavior of members is wholly unguided by any shared understandings of the situation and the kinds of action which are appropriate. It is extremely difficult to do so. Most groups which appear at first glance to be unstructured (such as many newly-formed groups) are only relatively so. Their members quickly discover that they agree enough on what behavior is called for to begin the development of a more explicit organization.

Culture both gives direction to on-going behavior and at the same time arises out of it. Speaking of norms (as a part of culture) Homans puts it this way:

If we can think of a norm as a goal that a group wishes to reach, we can see that the goal is not set up, like the finish line of a race, before the race starts, but rather that the group decides, after it starts running, what the finish line will be. Once the norm is established, it exerts a back effect on the group.[8]

Some degree of order and predictability in human behavior, both individually and collectively, is so critically important as to be a prerequisite for survival. We observe that in any situation in which individuals interact they will ordinarily do so in ways already organized for them by the culture they have collectively brought into the situation, and, where necessary, they will create new standardized ways of coping with one another and the environment. Culture as the arbiter of what is fitting and necessary in behavior and behavior itself are irrevocably intertwined, each a function of the other, each a source of both stability and change in the other. As it is sometimes put, the two are in a state of dynamic tension. Overt social behavior is never wholly determined by culture and its departures from the script may ultimately alter the script itself. Yet behavior cannot escape the modelling influence of culture.

SOME OTHER FEATURES
OF SOCIOLOGY'S OUTLOOK

Like every scholarly field, sociology has some identifying features which are not, perhaps, essential to a minimum definition, yet are very much part of it. Some development of these additional characteristics will help to get a better "feel" of how it is to think sociologically about behavior.

Looking Beyond the Obvious

The professional posture of a sociologist requires him to stand apart from his subject matter, to detach himself and step outside the ongoing social scene in which he ordinarily participates like anyone else. He is a little like the drama critic who must write a review of a new play after its first performance. The critic sets

[8] Homans, *op. cit.*, p. 126.

aside the point of view of an ordinary audience member in order to analyze the structure of the play, its content, staging, and the performances of the actors. Unlike the sociologist, however, the drama critic will usually also pass judgment on the quality of the play, while the sociologist tries to exclude value judgments from his analyses of social behavior.

The special nature of his interest causes the sociologist to look for and to see different things (or to see the same things in different ways) than the engaged participants. In a provocative discussion of this point Berger used the phrase "looking behind the façades" of social structures.[4] Here is a group whose members resent Bill's "bossy" behavior. A sociological observer notices almost at once that the admired leader of the group often acts in the same way as Bill (a low-ranking member), but the other members are not antagonized by the leader. The sociologist "sees" that the hostility of the members is produced not so much by the nature of Bill's behavior as by its incompatibility with his rank in the group.

The organization of behavior which is the sociologist's province is almost never immediately clear in the social scene as it appears to the people engaged in it. Therefore, the sociologist is always probing "below," "behind," "through" the immediate circumstances for the structure that is there. This is as true of the organization of a casual conversation among friends as it is of the most portentous social structures which exist.

The Sociologist as Skeptic

The sociologist is inevitably cast in the role of skeptic. He cannot help being skeptical of the easy answers people have learned to give for complex problems of social behavior. There cannot be a single sociologist who has not frequently listened while friends or acquaintances happily revealed their confusions and misunderstandings about a problem he recognizes as essentially sociological in character. The friend, of course, will not be discomfited in the least, since like most of the general public he has no idea of what sociology is, and it will not occur to him that the

[4] P. L. Berger, *Invitation to Sociology*, Garden City: Doubleday & Co., Anchor Books, 1963, p. 32.

sociologist might have some special competence in the subject under discussion. Most specialists probably have this experience. Many an attorney has winced, no doubt, as a layman unknowingly revealed his misconceptions of the law.

But the sociologist's skepticism must not be thought of as wholly negative, an attitude which seeks the destruction of other men's cherished notions of reality. The point is that the sociologist has been trained to see a special class of problems in human behavior, and so he becomes highly sensitive to experiences in which the problem and the model applied to its understanding are mismatched. He finds that the answers given to sociological problems by others are sometimes not only inappropriate but terribly oversimplified as well.

Sociologists, particularly those who conduct original research, have a most healthy respect for the complexities of their subject matter. Nothing can be taken for granted, not even the most seductive generalizations of "common sense." The research sociologist is continually reminded of how little we know, scientifically speaking, about human behavior. He is aware that he and his colleagues are only pioneering in a small way on the edges of a trackless wilderness, whose size and complexity exceed the grasp of the imagination in almost the same sense that the human mind fails before the task of imaginatively laying hold of the physical universe revealed in modern physical science.

The practice of sociological research is not conducive to arrogance about knowledge of human affairs, but rather the converse. No wonder then that it is hard to capture the sociologist's mind with the routine formulas that society uses in its attempts to cope with social problems large or small. At the same time, if he is a wise man as well as a sociologist, he will not be contemptuous of men's fumbling efforts to solve pressing problems since he will recognize that his own ability to do so is still strictly limited. The problems of the day cannot wait. They must be dealt with somehow. So he may cheerfully participate as a citizen in efforts to improve the human condition, even as he remains a skeptic, intellectually speaking. But back within his disciplinary perspective he will know vividly at times the mystery of human behavior, even the most ordinary behavior. His objective is to penetrate that mystery, and perhaps to reduce it a little.

The Reality of Social Phenomena

Another aspect of the sociological orientation toward man is its assumption that social phenomena are "real." This deserves comment because newcomers to the discipline have difficulty with this point. "You can see an individual but you can't see a social organization" seems to be the way many students feel about the matter. Social organization which links two or more persons somehow has a lesser, more ephemeral kind of reality than events located within individuals.

By contrast, the "reality" of biological and psychological phenomena seems less tenuous and needs no demonstration to most persons. Each of us experiences them subjectively, and the temptation is to regard social and cultural data as merely summations of the acts and characteristics of individuals. After all, are not groups made up of individuals? We are easily persuaded by this line of reasoning or something similar to it. On the other hand, a review of what has been said in this chapter about alternative perspectives for abstracting from the totality of human behavior may give some food for thought here. Each of the conceptual perspectives ingenious man has invented in the effort to understand himself pictures part, but *only* part of "reality." Each leaves out more than it includes. Without going over familiar ground again, it may be helpful to this discussion of the "reality" of social phenomena to consider an example or two of this abstracting (and therefore excluding) aspect of models.

Take a familiar word like "personality," a part of everyday speech and a macro-concept in psychology. Its familiarity conceals its ambiguity. The reader is invited to attempt a serious definition of this term, one he has certainly used hundreds of times, no doubt with full confidence that he knows what he means by it. On reflection one might decide that personality is certain qualities the person has, such as "friendly," "talkative," or "self-confident." But these qualities are assumed to be somehow within a person only because someone else has observed his behavior and made the inference that *behind the behavior is something* that produces it. What is that something? Another observer (or the same observer in a different situation) might find quite different qualities in the person. Psychologists have devised many methods for quantitatively describing personality. But an individual's *score* on the Minnesota Multiphasic Personality Inventory or the *protocol* resulting from his exposure to the Rorschach test is surely not his personality. We must assume that personality is "that which produces the test performance." But what is it? After all, different tests seem to be getting at rather different kinds of things.

Different definitions of personality exist and may be perfectly acceptable in different circumstances. Our intention is not to choose a "correct" definition, but to show that any conception of personality, carefully examined, involves a linguistic agreement among a number of persons to let a word stand for phenomena whose existence is largely *inferred*. What confounds us here is the tendency to confuse the human body with the human personality, hence to base our faith in the reality of the latter on inappropriate grounds. Despite our conviction that personality is real, it (however we conceive it) cannot be seen, touched, heard, or tasted. The biological organism, on the other hand, can impinge in this direct way on our senses. To be succinct, what we can see is an organism in action; personality cannot be directly observed.

The psychologist's definition of personality differs from the layman's in its greater precision. Sometimes this very explicitness offends the layman. "But your definition eludes the real essence of personality as I understand it," he may tell the psychologist. The best response to this complaint is probably to suggest that, since all definitions are arbitrary, the doubter is perfectly free to come up with his own. All behavioral scientists are familiar with the resistance created when a familiar word, richly laden with connotations, is used as a scientific concept with a barer but more precise meaning. To the scientist, the value of a concept is not determined by whether it "feels right" or not, but by its utility in helping to understand the behavior in which he is interested. If it works in this sense, he is not likely to worry much about the "reality" of the phenomena symbolized by the concept.

All this is not to suggest for a moment that the idea of a personality is a linguistic illusion. Plenty of evidence suggests that headway can be made in understanding some kinds of behavior (not all, of course) by assuming that part of each individual is an organized set of tendencies to respond which is conveniently labelled "personality."

The word "group" is another term everyone knows, and it is also a central concept in sociology. It is every bit as slippery as personality. Of necessity the sociologist uses the term with greater care and explicitness than does the layman. Just as psychologists have produced many definitions of personality, there are many sociological definitions of group. Many definitions of the word consistent with the sociological frame of reference may be acceptable to the sociologist, depending upon circumstances.

To illustrate, a sociologist might chart the flow of communication between group members over a series of meetings, noting how it is distributed both quantitatively and qualitatively among members over time. When repetitive patterns appear in this record he might say: "The group is the patterned interaction among these people, that and nothing more." [5] Not the physical appearance, facial expressions, emotions, or other attributes of 'the members, just the *pattern of interaction* which links their actions. It is immaterial to him that these same people engage in different interaction patterns in other settings. He may care little about their motivations. He looks for the orderliness which characterizes their behavior when they are together and influenced by being together. In short, he abstracts some aspects of human behavior out of the whole which is present, an intellectual operation which is the logical equivalent of the psychologist studying personality.

Finally, groups as seen by sociologists are neither more nor less real than personalities. However defined, both concepts have referents which must be inferred rather than directly observed. All we can ever see is one or more separate physical organisms engaged in diverse acts. The structure of psychological tendencies that *is* personality is invisible. Similarly, the structure of interpersonal acts which *is* the group is invisible. Both concepts require an abstraction of different things out of the same whole.

[5] This particular approach is in common use among sociological students of the small group. One of the more influential examples is presented in R. F. Bales, *Interaction Process Analysis*. Reading, Mass.: Addison-Wesley Publishing Co., 1950.

So the sociologist would hold that the units of his science (groups, associations, institutions, communities, societies, and others) may as profitably be assumed to refer to aspects of reality as the units of other sciences.[6] To them may be applied the same test used by other sciences: whether when employed in accordance with the scientific method they help to account for the observable behavior we seek to understand.

SOCIOLOGY AND SCIENCE

A few words should be said about sociology as a science. Not all sociologists agree that their discipline is now a science or can reasonably hope to become one in the future. Still, a substantial majority today are committed to the view that sociology is best developed as a science, and this fact colors the discipline's perspective and contributes some of its characteristic features. Here it is not important to review the debate over this point. If most sociologists act on the assumption that their field is a science or is in process of becoming one, then the character of their work will ultimately settle the argument.

Those who link sociology with the larger scientific community regard the common tendency to equate science with particular subject matters as a vulgar misunderstanding of the nature of science. A more sophisticated view recognizes that science is defined not by a particular range of natural phenomena, but by a method of securing reliable knowledge about any natural phenomena. Most readers will by now be acquainted with some of the many statements of the scientific method; there is no need to go into the matter here. We may simply say that, like other sciences (or would-be sciences if the reader prefers), sociology seeks ultimately the development of theories which are empirically supported or supportable. In the end the facts are the test of the theories, not the reverse. Sociology stands ready to alter or jettison its theories if evidence requires it.

As in other sciences, it occasionally happens that a particular

[6] For an interesting discussion of the reality of groups, see C. K. Warriner, "Groups Are Real: A Reaffirmation," *American Sociological Review*, 21, 1956, pp. 549–554.

scholar becomes emotionally committed to a theory and cannot modify or lay it aside in the face of the facts. In such cases the man probably does not know that his judgment is impaired, a different situation from deliberate intellectual dishonesty. The latter does occur in rare instances; it is the worst of all scholarly sins. Both possibilities remind us of the distinction between the values and procedures of a scientific discipline (a kind of social organization, by the way) and the complex, fallible human beings who develop and maintain the discipline. Science provides correctives for the mistakes of scientists, but of course cannot insure that no mistakes will be made.[7]

Sociology's primary search is for basic knowledge rather than the short-run solution of social problems, although nothing prevents the application of sociological knowledge to practical affairs where relevant. For those interested, lengthy and interesting discussions of the problems and possibilities of social science are readily available.[8]

THE SOCIOLOGIST AS A PERSON

It may occur to the reader that the sociologist's way of looking at behavior could be a formidable burden to its owner and a threat to the people around him. It must be tiresome for the sociologist to be always seeing social systems in action and having to analyze them as he goes through life. He can never relax and just enjoy life! And what about his friends and associates? Don't

[7] Drama and tragedy are implicit in the potential conflict between the austere dedication to truth required by science and the complex, contradictory strivings of flesh-and-blood men and women who link their personal fates with a scientific discipline. The theme has lately attracted literary people, no doubt because of the looming importance of science in the modern world. Aspects of the conflict are treated interestingly in the novels of C. P. Snow. See especially, *The Affair*. New York: Charles Scribner's Sons, 1960. Another example is Eleazar Lipsky, *The Scientists*. New York: Appleton-Century-Crofts, 1959.

[8] Among many possibilities, see D. Lerner (ed.), *The Human Meaning of the Social Sciences*. New York: Meridian Books, 1959. Also M. Natanson (ed.), *Philosophy of the Social Sciences: A Reader*. New York: Random House, 1963.

they have reason to fear his observation, with its capacity to "see behind the façades?" Attitudes like this grow up around all specialized students of human behavior; especially clear examples are furnished by physicians, psychologists, and psychiatrists. These attitudes are compounded of respect (for learning) and fear (of threatening applications of specialized knowledge). Ambivalence in public images reveals itself in the hardily perennial stories of their short-comings, such as the gleeful accounts of psychologists and their maladjusted children. The comparative scarcity of such tales about sociologists reflects the relative popular ignorance of what sociology is about.

A misunderstanding here can be cleared up by using the sociologist as example. His way of looking at behavior is highly specialized, and its acquisition requires disciplined training and practice. But the sociologist as a person is never wholly contained in his professional role. When he goes to work it is as though he dons an invisible pair of intellectual glasses through which he peers until his task of the moment is finished. Afterwards, off come the glasses, and the sociologist is at once an engaged and committed participant in the life going on around him, like anyone else.

In other words, sociologists do not always look at human behavior from their professional perspective any more than do physicians, biologists, economists, or other specialists. It is not a matter of choice or taste. It is a matter of inevitability, partly because the sociological model, like any other, is germane in some circumstances but not in others, and partly because the sociologist is unable to be coldly rational and objective at all times. True, his conduct as an ordinary citizen may sometimes partly reflect knowledge that comes from his discipline, just as an attorney in his private life may make decisions partly on the basis of his legal expertise. But very frequently his actions do not reflect his special knowledge, even where it is relevant, while it will always be influenced by other considerations. Consequently, the sociological perspective, like other valid models, when wisely used is intellectually liberating, not constricting. And the sociologist's friends need not be uncomfortable or apprehensive around him. The one thing he most certainly does *not* do is subject his relationships with other people to a detached, professional analysis. His friends will find him as vain or modest, as impulsive or predictable, as wise or foolish as anyone else they know.

USING THE SOCIOLOGICAL
PERSPECTIVE

An English-speaking person would like to be able to converse in German, and to that end he carefully studies a German grammar. Unless he supplements this work with extensive *practice* in speaking German his investment is largely wasted. This same point cannot be too heavily stressed with respect to the acquisition of a *working knowledge* of the sociological orientation toward human conduct. The valuable contribution this point of view can make to anyone's intellectual equipment can never be realized solely by reading even the best sociological treatises. In addition, the abstract model must be brought to life by acquiring something of the sociologist's habits of thought in the social arena as he observes human behavior.

Human social behavior is simply there, to be understood or not, from one or perhaps several vantage points. Not until a person has, through practice, acquired the special sensitivity and at least a few of sociology's rudimentary conceptual tools can he bring them into play automatically at the right times and places. Then, and only then, does the whole subject move out of the textbooks into a person's life, giving him sharp new insights from time to time, moments when he knows he is seeing more deeply into reality than he could before.

The empirical facts a student meets in sociology courses are important aids in gaining a clear picture of particular manifestations of social organization, and they are the raw material with which the sociologist works. But there are countless thousands of these facts. Nobody can remember them for long, and many have a way of getting out of date rather rapidly. However, the underlying perspective which informs the discipline of sociology can be applied in *any socially organized situation whatever*. It is not a set of facts, it is a way of looking at facts. Once mastered, it will outlive and transcend any specific collection of facts. The perspective can be applied very usefully indeed by the amateur as well as the professional sociologist.

The mind-broadening potential of sociology's perspective need not be restricted to the professional sociologist. Like other valuable frames of reference for comprehending the human scene, it is available to anyone willing to make the effort to acquire it. But conscientious practice in its use, as well as study of its character, is really indispensable.

Seriously, then, it is suggested that the reader may find it profitable in his own interest to seek occasions for applying this new frame of reference as well as he can. This may be done in many different ways, and almost any sociology course will suggest situations to be used for this purpose, as well as ways of *conceptualizing* social organization. As a starter, one can watch for occasions in which, without appearing conspicuous, he can quietly disengage his mind from full participation in a social scene in order to search for its underlying social structure. He can, for instance, try putting the participants in rank order of frequency of communications sent to others and received from others, noting the degree to which such rank orders are stable. Then he might try to determine the typical patterns of who talks to whom. After this he can try to answer the question: how is prestige distributed in this group? Or again, and more complex because it involves inference, he can attempt to describe the roles of group members, thinking of roles as patterned descriptions of expected behavior rather than actual behavior. How many fairly clear-cut roles (not how many persons) are there? To what extent is there agreement on the content of these roles? Which persons seem to behave most often in accordance with the role prescriptions and which the least? What happens when someone's behavior departs from role prescriptions? Patient practice along such lines will at first be disappointing, but gradually will lead to a more clear perception of what social organization is and to a more appreciative grasp of its great significance in human affairs.

A married person can ask himself: where did the components of the husband and wife roles in my marriage come from? What are the oldest and newest elements? What parts are really specific to this marriage; what parts are shared with other married couples? Where is the greatest compatibility and incompatibility in husband's and wife's conceptions of the two roles, and what are the sources? If he is a young person he can compare the marital roles in his marriage with those found in a marriage of an elderly couple he knows. If he should try to explain the differences on grounds other than just "age" how could this be done in sociological terms?

As one gradually becomes sensitized to the sociological model questions will arise concerning dozens of events in the passing scene. During a political campaign the question of how people come to voting decisions may arise. The usual assumptions underlying campaign techniques may seem questionable, and the student can discover that sociologists have learned a good deal here. He reads in the newspaper that American swimming coaches attribute much of their spectacular recent success to the fact that they are developing their young swimmers in homogeneous age groups. What may be involved here? Or again in the area of sports, he may ponder the question: in what sense is a football coach at least as much an applied sociologist as an applied psychologist? Careful scrutiny of a football game from a sociological vantage point can be surprisingly interesting and revealing.

Anyone who seeks conscientious practice of the sociological perspective needs a nodding acquaintance with a few of the basic conceptual tools which enable sociologists to translate the broad orientation into specific observations. Most readers of this book will have what is necessary, or any introductory textbook will do quite well for the purpose. As in learning a foreign language, results come slowly at first. It isn't reasonable to expect the power of this new intellectual resource to reveal itself at once. But those who persist will begin to know delight and satisfaction as the searchlight which seems at first so clumsy begins to light up the landscape and disclose things that were there all the time but not seen.

THE SOCIAL PSYCHOLOGICAL MODEL

Before we complete this chapter a brief mention of the perspective of social psychology is essential. The reason is that many scholars identify themselves as both sociologists and social psychologists. The two fields can and should be conceptually distinguished from each other, but to a considerable extent work is done in both fields by the same men. We can be brief because the main focus is on sociology, and also because the social psychologist with sociological training will have the sociological perspective available to him as he engages in social psychological studies.

Social psychology is a hybrid discipline, nurtured by several fields but particularly by sociology and psychology. It is nicely symbolic of this parentage that the first two texts in social psychology, so named, were published in 1908, one by a sociologist, E. A. Ross, the other by a psychologist, W. McDougall.[9] From the earliest days of sociology, some of its scholars have been deeply interested in problems of a social psychological nature. In the 1959 directory of members of the American Sociological Association social psychology was the single area of specialization listed more frequently than any other. Hinkle and Hinkle, writing in 1954, held that

> Throughout the last half-century American sociologists have adhered to an individualistic conception of social life. They have generally viewed all social groups as pluralities of associating and interacting individuals whose psychic nature is the ultimate source of social change.[10]

This generalization is so broad as to overlook the other strain in sociological thought which visualizes organized social behavior in somewhat the manner described earlier in this chapter. In the writer's opinion the years since World War II have seen a clarification among American sociologists of the distinction between the social psychological and sociological points of view. They are not the same. To confuse them is, in the last analysis, to concede that sociology has no unique disciplinary orientation, but is a branch of psychology. There may be a few sociologists who feel that this is the case, but not many.

[9] E. A. Ross, *Social Psychology: An Outline and Sourcebook.* New York: Macmillan, 1908. W. McDougall, *Introduction to Social Psychology.* London: Methuen, 1908.
[10] R. C. Hinkle, Jr., and G. J. Hinkle, *The Development of Modern Sociology,* Short Studies in Sociology Series. New York: Random House, 1954, p. 14.

An abstract and more or less logical definition of a learned field and its characteristics does not necessarily describe for us all the professional labors of the actual persons identified with it. At any rate, it is not possible to describe what the body of American sociologists does without including reference to social psychology.

Social psychology's subject matter is the relationship between the behavior and psychological characteristics of individuals and their sociocultural environment. This broad statement says nothing about the nature or direction of the relationship. Consider the behavior of the members of a particular American family, and suppose that we are interested in the mother. The social psychologist may seek a partial explanation of her behavior in the impact upon her of the behavior of the other family members. The mother's conduct is the "dependent" variable, as it were, while the activities of other members constitute the "independent" variables. The social psychologist may also note the effects of family roles, transmitted from the culture through the experience of this particular family, with variations from the cultural pattern of greater or lesser significance. Seen this way, the family group and the family institution are part of the sociocultural environment of the individual, and the social psychologist is of course committed to the study of organism-environment relationships.

But the social psychologist may also primarily focus in this example not on the mother or any other single family member but on the social structure of the family unit. Rather than ask how he can understand the behavior of one member by reference to the others, he may seek partial explanation of the group structure by reference to the psychological characteristics of its members. He will recognize other "causes" of the social structure than this, of course, just as in the previous case there will be diverse causes of the mother's behavior. But here the group structure is treated as the "dependent" variable and psychological characteristics become "independent." The first problem is somewhat more psychological in nature, in that knowledge of individual behavior is sought, the second is more sociological since a social system is the object of inquiry. In both, the characteristics of the individual are explicitly taken into account. Social psychologists readily enter into both kinds of investigation. This is increasingly true whether the social scientist was trained primarily as a psychologist or as a sociologist. There remain some recognizable differences in approach, but these need not detain us here. It is noteworthy that both the American Sociological Association and the American Psychological Association have special sections in social psychology.

As the social psychologist sees it, the person responds to and is molded by social pressures, but at the same time actively reaches out into the social world to make it yield adequate satisfaction of his own wants. Specific illustrations can be found in the extensive work done by "sociological" social psychologists on the self concept, and, more recently, on achievement motivation. In both these examples the researcher and theorist is explicitly interested in psychological structures within the individual as well as their sociocultural origins and consequences.

SUMMARY

This chapter has attempted to communicate something of the sociological perspective on human behavior. It has *not* dealt with the manner in which sociologists divide their complicated field of study into various subjects, nor has it had anything to say about the findings of sociologists as they go about their research tasks. Further, it has not acquainted the student with the great contributors to this discipline, nor has it presented any information about how sociologists have organized themselves as a discipline of scholars to safeguard and advance their professional interests. These and other matters have been subordinated to a difficult but important task: communicating what is unique about the manner in which the sociologist views human behavior.

Over the centuries man has constructed and made use of many generalized perspectives or models to help him in understanding himself and his environment. Sociology is a late addition to this supply of intellectual tools. Among the scientific models applied to human behavior each has something useful to add to our store of reliable knowledge. Problems arise when attempts are made to use inappropriate models for given circumstances. Perhaps this applies particularly to sociology, since its point of view is novel in intellectual history and unfamiliar to most persons in our society. Everyone is familiar with social behavior, it is true, but very few have acquired the sociologist's way of thinking about it. The result is that nonsociological models are frequently applied or misapplied to sociological problems.

Quite simply, the sociological orientation is concerned with all human behavior which is socioculturally organized. It is interested in the kind and degree of organization, in the problems of stability and change in social organization, and in the relationship between overt social behavior and the culture patterns relevant to actual performance. All this may be stated differently, of course, but it describes very generally what distinguishes this field from all others. As a discipline, sociology has no greater intrinsic interest in one particular kind of social organization than another (as do several other social sciences). It is not focussed on the individual as the primary unit of its orientation. Allied as it is with the scientific community, sociology seeks truth first in its sphere of competence. The application of sociological knowledge, whether by sociologists or others, is perfectly acceptable and for many may constitute the field's reason for existence, but application takes second place to the search for truth. In their employment of the sociological perspective sociologists probe below the level of social behavior as ordinarily experienced. Since the surface manifestations of behavior conceal the structure and process in which they are primarily interested they may properly be called skeptics concerning the usual interpretations of social phenomena, though not in a cynical or destructive sense. Their professional posture requires them to stand aside from personal involvement with the objects of their study so far as this is possible. At the same time, when off-duty, so to speak, they live their personal lives as other men do, full of complexity, contradiction, passion, and foolishness, illuminated occasionally, one hopes, with clear insight and wisdom.

Too much familiarity and the trivia of our daily rounds dulls our imagination when it comes to that strange animal, man. Out of the myriad forms life has taken on this lonely planet, only one species has evolved the capacity to become aware of itself and curious about its condition and destiny. "The unexamined life is not worth living," Socrates said. What an anthropocentric statement! It could never occur to a single one of the billions of lives found in other species. All except man are locked in their organic prisons. Only man speaks, is curious, and creates culture. Man alone reflects on the world and himself and because of this weeps or is exalted. What fascinates man most of all is man. Restlessly he seeks to know himself. With the passing centuries his power to do so has slowly grown. In the very recent past it has occurred to him that the method of science, so immensely productive of reliable knowledge in other spheres, may perhaps be applied to the study of man, taking its place alongside older pathways to self-knowledge. Sociology has begun to write one of the chapters in that story.

II

WHAT DO SOCIOLOGISTS STUDY?

In Chapter I it was said that sociology "is concerned with how human social behavior is organized, and how this organization changes over time." That chapter's elaboration of this and other defining statements may help to communicate in a very general way the sociologist's special perspective on human behavior. To emphasize the unique contribution this discipline can make to man's understanding of himself, this writer would prefer to apply the word "sociological" only to scholarly work which is informed by this fundamental orientation. We say this in full realization that a great many sociologists are *also* social psychologists or sometimes work within basic orientations more closely allied with other disciplines. Social psychology is a special case in that, for historical reasons, sociologists can claim a share of it as can several other fields, notably psychology.

Many things distinguish one science of human behavior from another. Some are important, others trivial. Today there is a good deal of overlapping of the work done in several fields. This is inevitable and desirable. Still, what was called the "sociological perspective" in Chapter I is the critical identifying characteristic of sociology. We may put the point like this. It is quite possible that, a century from now, the scientific study of human behavior will be pursued under rather different labels from those familiar today. Nevertheless, the sociological perspective will be present (along with others equally fundamental) under whatever name appears most appropriate to our descendants.

We now must be a bit more explicit about what sociologists study. In a way, every introductory textbook does this job, and can devote far more space to the matter than can be afforded here. However, as always in this book, we are not talking sociology but talking *about* it. So we shall not present the results of sociological investigation but rather try to clarify the ways in which human social behavior is divided, so to speak, in order to bring the discipline's orientation to bear on problems of manageable size.

The task is not easy, because no simple, rational scheme for partitioning the subject matter of sociology has achieved general acceptance by sociologists themselves. Introductory texts sometimes unwittingly convey the impression that work done in the field has an overall logic and symmetry of development which in fact it has not. Actually, this province of learning, reflecting both historical and contemporary forces, is turbulent, very rapidly changing, hence somewhat disorganized.

Nevertheless, we will shortly attempt to set forth a simple description of the principal areas of sociological investigation. Before doing so, a brief review of historical factors influencing the present organization of the field will aid in understanding the present state of affairs.

A GLANCE AT THE HISTORY
OF AMERICAN SOCIOLOGY

For reasons of space, we must be content with a few observations which help to grasp the influence of the past on present notions of the proper task of the sociologist. While something like a sociological view of behavior has occasionally been utilized over almost the whole history of Western thought, sociology in America slowly began to take form in the latter half of the nineteenth century. Among the forces which attended its birth and helped form its character were the heady doctrine of evolution, a widespread belief in the inevitability of human progress, and faith that progress could be hastened by the application of human intelligence operating through knowledge of natural laws. In addition, men of sensitivity and conscience were appalled by the abuses attending early industrialization and urbanization and felt that something should and could be done to relieve human suffering.

Although there was nothing in the new evolutionary thought which *required* an optimistic application to society, most frequently (with a conspicuous exception in William Graham Sumner) early American sociologists, and French and English too, managed a firm belief that the pathway of man was not only onward but upward as well. There would seem to be conflict between belief in deterministic natural laws governing the behavior of men and faith that men could improve their state by their own efforts. Still, most sociologists managed to rationalize, ignore, or otherwise live with this conflict. Optimism about man was, after all, a strong component in the intellectual climate of that time. Belief in both the possibility of a science or sciences of man and its utility for improving human welfare came easily enough. The exciting new discoveries and applications of physical science were everywhere evident, and perhaps it needed little more than imagination and an act of will to produce the same results with man himself.

Hinkle and Hinkle point out that another characteristic of American sociology from its early days was its tendency to see society as originating in and sustained by the psychological characteristics of individuals.[1] This psychologistic tendency helps to account for the long-term interest of so many sociologists in the hybrid discipline of social psychology.

Early in the twentieth century the work of most leading sociologists represented in varying degrees all the characteristics mentioned. In both Europe and America the task of developing the new science typically took the form of writing major treatises, or sociological systems, which set forth on a rather grand scale the authors' conceptions of social structure and social process. These are ambitious works, but the painstaking accumulation of empirical evidence usually associated with the development of a

[1] R. C. Hinkle, Jr., and G. J. Hinkle, *The Development of Modern Sociology.* New York: Random House, 1954, pp. 14–17.

science played little part in them. The process of systematically gathering and testing information had scarcely begun. Meanwhile, these pioneers were anxious to get on with the task of understanding society in scientific terms. A number of them were brilliant men whose germinal ideas still command the respect of later scholars. Yet from today's vantage point it can be seen that in some respects they attempted too much too soon.

In some of these works, along with the effort to construct a scientific sociological system of thought, we also find concern with the social utility of the new discipline, a faith that it could be used to ameliorate social problems, and also the generally psychologistic tone mentioned above.

World War I and its aftermath considerably diminished the buoyant optimism of sociologists and of intellectuals generally. Utopia suddenly seemed much further off, much more difficult to achieve, and not so easily even defined. In the face of enormously destructive, irrational events and forces, the promises of rationality embodied in social science seemed much more problematical. At the same time more and more sociologists began to realize that a science, properly so called, could not be created at once through essentially deductive reasoning alone by even the most brilliant minds. The conviction rapidly spread through the young discipline that inductive reasoning based on the patient, careful accumulation of empirical evidence was essential if truly scientific accounts of human social behavior were ever to be achieved.

As a result, in the years following the war, sociologists became much less interested in social amelioration and in the production of ambitious theoretical systems of sociological thought. The new profession of social work was also evolving (sharing some of its historical roots with sociology). The distinction between sociology and social work became clearer. Many graduate schools of social work, in fact, evolved out of and away from early university departments of sociology. Sociologists became increasingly explicit about seeing their own task as the development of a basic scholarly discipline, *not* its application to the relief of human misery. It would be up to the applied professions to make whatever use was feasible of sociological findings. Sociologists themselves should remain as "value-free" as possible, and there were many disputes about the degree to which this was indeed possible.

In any case, they turned vigorously to the systematic collection of social facts, and became increasingly uncomfortable with high-level abstract generalizations unsupported by evidence. Concurrent with the new emphasis on empirical research was a growing differentiation of the field into specialized parts and an increasing preoccupation with research methodology. After all, it was not feasible to do detailed factual investigations of social units as large as the entire society. It was necessary to work within smaller frames.

This growing specialization received explicit recognition in the program of the American Sociological Society in 1921.[2] Some of the new fields of investigation, such as social change, community structure, and social stratification, reflected the fundamental subject matter concerns of a general science of sociology. Others, such as delinquency and crime, community social problems, and educational problems, continued (in a more detached and objective context) the earlier interest in social reform and human betterment. Social psychology began to emerge more clearly as an endeavor bridging sociology and psychology but not coterminous with either.

More and more attention was paid to the development of valid and reliable techniques for gathering and interpreting social data. It became increasingly clear that, along with more traditional and informal methods, sociologists would have to invest heavily in statistical methodology. Specific training in research techniques became an essential part of training for the field.

These are some of the trends which characterized the development of sociological subject matter between the two world wars. The second war serves as a rough date for several further developments leading into the contemporary period, although actually these came gradually. One of the most important was a fresh interest in sociological theory. Almost like a swinging pendulum, the field had turned sharply away from general theory after World War I. For a generation the field was so immersed in fact collection that this sometimes seemed to become an end in itself. As mountains of social data piled up it became rather clear that unless the

[2] Hinkle and Hinkle, *op. cit.*, pp. 20–21.

new evidence was correlated with theoretical work, serving both to test theory and suggest avenues for its extension, the science could not be advanced. Sociology could fail to develop if it was over-preoccupied with theory without related research, but it could also fail if it bogged down in fact-collecting without determining the implications of fact for theory.

So the pendulum moved back in the opposite direction. Today the old hostile dichotomy between theory and research has pretty well disappeared. A generation or two ago, a creative sociologist might well be labelled either a "theorist" or a "researcher." This was likely to imply almost completely different interests. Today, the innovating sociologist is normally expected to set his empirical research in a meaningful framework of theory in such a way as to advance the development of theory. By the same token, he is expected to subject his theoretical ideas to empirical test.

The revival of interest in sociological theory has given fresh impetus to the influence of major European writers such as the Italian Vilfredo Pareto, the Frenchman Émile Durkheim, and the German Max Weber. Their influence (particularly that of Durkheim and Weber) is easily traced in the work of major American theorists of this generation. But sociological thought in the postwar period has not returned to the development of massive, deductively built systems of thought divorced from empirical research. The present vogue is for more modest theories at a level of inclusiveness and complexity appropriate to the currently available kit of research tools. The technical sophistication of research methodology has made great strides and this plus the new electronic methods of data analysis (backed by much more adequate research funds than hitherto) has made it feasible for sociologists to undertake relatively thorough and subtle quantitative tests of theoretical ideas.

The proliferation of special subject matter areas has continued. Simultaneously there appears to be a clearer conception of sociology as a general science of social behavior whose principles are applicable to innumerable specific social settings, and something like consensus that the field's main task is its development as a generalizing science. Thus, although one sociologist may work largely in industrial locations, another in hospitals, a third in the field of religion, all see their most important task as the illumination of their special area by application of the general principles of sociology, and conversely, the advancement of sociological knowledge by their studies in a particular segment of social organization.

Some change has also occurred in the prevailing notions of the relationship between sociological science and its practical application. The tendency to feel that the discipline ought to be value-free and ought to avoid any sort of entanglement with practical or controversial issues has been modified. Sociologists are no longer so confident that it is possible to keep their own work devoid of implicit value judgments, nor so likely to be troubled by the implications for social policy that their investigations may have. There is, perhaps, a growing recognition that sociology could not develop without the support of society, and an admission (sometimes reluctant) that it must in some sense "earn" its support here and now (rather than in some distant future) by demonstrating the utility of what sociologists know.

Then too, just as the use of early psychological tests in World War I introduced psychology to the arena of practical affairs, the social research done in the armed forces during World War II wakened important sectors of society to the potential usefulness of behavioral science generally. Subsequently, sociologists have been sought by influential persons and organizations in government, industry, and elsewhere, often with offerings of financial support for needed research. This has been a powerful force moving sociology away from complete preoccupation with its development as a basic science.

At present the view of many professional sociologists is probably something like this. The most important long-run responsibility and goal is the development of sociology as a "pure" or basic science. At the same time it is acceptable (and often unavoidable from the standpoint of research support) for sociologists to engage in research which has direct bearing on the solution of practical problems, provided only that the individual does not compromise the rigid intellectual honesty and objectivity required of him as a scientist.

However sketchily, what has been said thus far indicates how sociology emerged from a particular historical background, continued to respond to contemporary forces, yet steadily matured as sociologists over several generations acquired a firmer conception of the discipline's subject matter and role in the larger society. Retrospectively it can be seen that the characteristics of the field developed naturally out of all that had gone before. The subject matter of sociology today still bears signs of its beginnings in the late nineteenth century, but many changes have taken place.

Some mention should be made of historical factors whose influence seems quite fortuitous. Sociology's subject matter can be defined in a way that is logical and clear. Yet when we look at the *actual* allocation of the field's resources in research and in teaching too, we find that their distribution hardly follows any logical plan. What sociologists are doing today reflects not only their own rational conception of the subject but also a number of "historical accidents" logically unrelated to the main line of development. Since these factors have some importance in understanding sociology's subject matter, illustrations will clarify the point.

It is a kind of historical accident that sociology has for decades been concerned with the scientific study of the family in America — as much or more so than any other field. Logically viewed, there is no more reason why sociologists should be in this position with respect to the family than with respect to the economic and political institutions. As it happened, however, economics and political science had preempted these areas of study, but no organized discipline had done the same for family life. Much later, sociologists began seriously to apply the special perspective of their discipline to economic and political settings. A similar example is the area called "demography." There appears to be no compelling reason why so much of the scientific study of population composition, distribution, and change should have taken place within the boundaries of sociology. It was simply an important subject not yet firmly claimed by any of the emerging social science fields.

A different sort of illustration is furnished by what is sometimes called "small group sociology." In the earlier years of the discipline important concepts and ideas had been advanced by writers like Cooley and Simmel, and pioneering empirical studies had been done by such workers as Thrasher.[3] Still, serious scientific investigations by sociologists in this important area had undeniably languished for years. Then, after World War II, the study of small social systems underwent a real renaissance in sociology. One of the most important influences in bringing this about was almost certainly the fact that a number of psychologists (particularly those identified with the term "group dynamics") began to do important studies of small groups.[4] This development brought back the attention of sociologists. After all, they could scarcely afford to relinquish this subject area to their psychological brethren!

Another example of the way in which the organization of sociological subject matter reflects influences not inherent in the character of the field itself is furnished by the changing interests of the larger society in what sociology has to offer. Medical sociology is a specialty that has grown dramatically in the last fifteen years. It has done so not because sociology needed to move in this direction but because the federal government invested very large sums of money in all kinds of medical research through the National Institutes of Health. Some of this money has been spent in the behavioral sciences, including sociology. There are even several graduate programs today which focus on the training of medical sociologists.

It has been an interesting and significant development. However, nothing about the fundamental goals of sociology required rapid expansion in the area of medicine but not in other important sectors of society where important unresolved problems remain. Very recently Congress has passed significant new legislation in the field of education. Among other things, it provides

[3] See C. H. Cooley, *Human Nature and the Social Order.* New York: Charles Scribner's Sons, 1902; *The Sociology of George Simmel*, translated and edited by K. Wolff. New York: Free Press, 1950; F. M. Thrasher, *A Study of 1,313 Gangs in Chicago.* Chicago: University of Chicago Press, 1927.
[4] The prime mover in this group was Kurt Lewin. Some idea of his work is communicated in K. Lewin, "Studies in Group Decision," in D. Cartwright and A. Zander, *Group Dynamics: Research and Theory.* New York: Harper and Row, 1953, pp. 287–301.

substantial sums for educational research of many kinds. It may be confidently predicted that educational sociology, which has had rather low esteem in the discipline for many years, will now become a quickly growing specialty commanding a steadily increasing proportion of sociological research effort.

Such illustrations are easy to find. They show that sociology is no more independent of the surrounding and supporting society than any other field of endeavor. Inevitably, the field and its adherents reflect the nature of the social milieu, and there is nothing inherently bad about this. At the same time, such facts of life can raise problems. It is incumbent upon sociologists to keep their central vision of a generalizing social science clearly before them despite external circumstances which limit their ability to allocate disciplinary resources in a purely logical, or even purely rational manner.

Undergraduate course offerings furnish a very poor description of the attention sociologists actually are giving to the various branches of their field. It may seem strange that this should be so. Briefly, it is true because undergraduate teaching is responsive to needs other than the training of sociologists and the development of the field's content. Most students in sociology courses are going into other occupations, and their work in sociology is part of their general educational background. At the same time, some courses become popular with students, and the demand for them does not reflect the relative importance of their subjects in the discipline as a whole. For these and other reasons undergraduate courses tend to become embedded in a curricular structure which is not very sensitive to the changing outlines of sociology. Ordinarily, the graduate curriculum reflects current subject matter a good deal more faithfully.

SOCIOLOGY'S SUBJECT MATTER

Without further excursions we turn to describing what it is that sociology studies. Inkeles, in his own valuable treatment of this subject, takes three approaches to definition, epitomized in the questions: "What did the founding fathers say?" "What are contemporary sociologists doing?" "What does reason suggest?" [5] We have already spoken briefly on the first question. The more explicit statement which follows is in part an answer to both the others, but particularly the third. It is mainly an attempt to set forth the continuing concerns of sociology as distinguished from the sometimes frequent changes in the amount of attention paid to various parts of the field.

If a degree of temerity is involved in the task it is not because there is no agreement among sociologists on what their field is about. Most would agree with Moore that sociology "is about patterned social relations, their consequences and interrelations, and their changes," [6] and with many other similar statements. In fact, a good deal of consensus probably exists when the field's content is described in considerably more specific terms. However, there is much less agreement about precisely how the provinces of sociology should be divided and labelled. It is perhaps an inevitable state of affairs in a young and rapidly evolving field of scholarship.

The Units Studied by Sociology

Patterns of interdependent behavior are the units sociologists study. These patterns can be and have been classified in many ways. One of the simplest and most helpful here is based primarily on comparative size and complexity. Here then is a list of units arranged from large to small, though the assumption of a decreasing size is only approximate, not strictly accurate.

Society • Among the many available definitions this one is typical: a society is "an aggregate of people that is self-sustaining, that has a definite location and a long duration, and that shares a way of life." [7] While in our time there has been a considerable growth of intersocietal organization, by and large the

[5] A. Inkeles, *What Is Sociology?*, Englewood Cliffs, N.J.: Prentice-Hall, 1964, p. 2.
[6] W. E. Moore, "The Whole State of Sociology," *American Sociological Review*, 24, 1959, p. 717.
[7] B. Berelson and G. A. Steiner, *Human Behavior, An Inventory of Scientific Findings.* New York: Harcourt, Brace & World, 1964, p. 587.

society is the most inclusive unit sociologists have studied.[8] True, some societies are very large and others comparatively tiny, and they differ in many other respects, but all constitute social organizations having in common at least the attributes contained in the definition. All the smaller and more specialized units listed below are contained within each society.

Institution • We do not depart radically from prevailing notions by defining an institution as an organized set of social rules and the corresponding social behavior whereby the members of a society come to grips with a related cluster of important and recurrent needs and problems. Obvious examples like economic, political, familial, and religious institutions come at once to mind. More complex societies may contain others such as educational, scientific, recreational, and aesthetic institutions. This is the first and foremost level at which sociologists visualize the differentiation into parts of the units called societies. Just as they assume that societies are worthy of analysis, so they hold that social institutions are entities with similar characteristics despite the differences among them within and between societies.

Community • Again, many definitions exist. In this instance we choose one presented by Rose. A community is "a spatially limited group in a society with its physical setting and institutions, having a common and unique set of culture patterns." [9] The term may be equated with such familiar things as villages, towns, cities, and metropolises. Communities and societies are like each other and different from the other units presented here in that they are both tied by definition to a specific geographical location.

Organization • Etzioni defines organizations as "social units (or human groupings) deliberately constructed and reconstructed to seek specific goals." [10] His next sentence helpfully exemplifies

---

[8] Interesting discussions of the need for sociological analysis on a level transcending the society are presented in a recent issue of the *American Journal of Sociology*. See W. E. Moore, "Global Sociology: The World as a Singular System"; R. Bierstedt, "Indices of Civilization"; P. A. Sorokin, "Comments on Moore's and Bierstedt's Papers," *American Journal of Sociology*, 71, 1966, pp. 475–492.
[9] A. M. Rose, *Sociology, The Study of Human Relations*, 2nd ed. New York: Knopf, 1965, p. 723.
[10] A. Etzioni, *Modern Organizations*. Englewood Cliffs, N.J.: Prentice-Hall, 1964, p. 3.

the concept. "Corporations, armies, schools, hospitals, churches, and prisons are included; tribes, classes, ethnic groups, friendship groups and families are excluded." [11] Clearly, a very wide variety of phenomena are embraced by this class of units. Yet they are different from institutions and communities. Religion as an institution is not the same as a local church (which is an organization), but the two are intimately related. Any local community shelters a large number of organizations, but the two kinds of units are different in character.

Social Class • A class is "an open aggregate or stratum of people with roughly similar ranking in the particular community or society." [12] It can be seen from this definition that classes are not organizations and that they may cut across the boundaries of communities and institutions. Implied in the definition is an hierarchical arrangement of these units based on their differential possession or control of valued attributes, privileges, or possessions.

Groups or Aggregates Sharing Widely Recognized Attributes Without Necessarily Implying Status Differences • Briefly, this class of units includes a goodly number which ordinarily would be treated separately by sociologists. Examples would be ethnic groups, occupations, males, females, age grades (for example, adolescents), all public colleges, and farm dwellers. While it ordinarily would be assumed that most such groups or aggregates would share some common elements of culture, and somewhat fewer would also have a sense of common identity, by no means all would constitute organizations. In some cases organizations might be present, and these would overlap the units earlier called organizations.

Small Groups • What we have in mind here is a set of social rules and the associated pattern of interaction which binds the behavior of a limited number of individuals into a structure. Exact upper limits of size cannot be specified, but are roughly determined by the possibility of face-to-face interaction among all members in the normal course of events. Small groups differ in many significant ways beyond the present purview. A football team, a nuclear family, a committee, an aircraft crew, a small college class, the Supreme Court of the United States, and a

[11] *Ibid.*, p. 3.
[12] Berelson and Steiner, *op. cit.*, p. 459.

group of men who play poker together once a week illustrate the diversity represented by this classification.

As here conceived, small groups are a fundamental substratum of social structure in all societies. Homans has suggested that civilizations grow out of the organizational potential developed in social life in small groups, and that when civilizations decay this is the level to which social organization returns.[13] Here the social life of man may be said to have an immortality denied the individual organism. All the larger forms which social structure may take will contain this level at which men communicate directly with one another in their efforts to satisfy individual and collective needs.

Roles • A role is a pattern of behavior associated with one or more members of some social system by the system members at large (and often by outsiders as well).[14] This definition is reasonably consistent with general usage. For the first time on this list we are dealing with a unit which is not a complete social system, only a part of one. The nuclear family roles of husband-father, wife-mother, and child illustrate this point as well as the concept itself. In the general sense of the word here, a role is all the behavior (prescribed and actual) regularly denoted by these familiar terms. Of course it is self-evident that the notion of a husband-father is meaningless except in reference to the other roles comprising the entire system. Nevertheless, for analysis it is possible to speak of this single role. A reasonable analogy would be the distinction between the study of a carburetor and a complete internal combustion engine. The "meaning" of the former cannot be divorced from the latter of which it forms an integral part; but it is sensible to speak of the construction and operation of the carburetor itself. Roles are major parts of the units named earlier.

Norms and Social Relationships • A norm is a social rule widely disseminated in some social system specifying in a limited context of action the behavior that is appropriate or required of one or more members. A social relationship is the actual interdependent

[13] G. C. Homans, *The Human Group*. New York: Harcourt, Brace, 1950, pp. 454–459.
[14] A. P. Bates and J. S. Cloyd, "Toward the Development of Operations for Defining Group Norms and Member Roles," *Sociometry,* 19, 1956, pp. 26–39.

behavior among system members which ensues in a limited context of action defined by a norm.

These definitions are chosen so as to make the units still smaller than roles. As a pattern of *prescribed* behavior a role is a bundle of norms. As a pattern of *actual* behavior a role is one side of a set of social relationships. In a particular family a single norm may prescribe that children should obey their parents. In overt conduct the social relationship coordinate with the norm would be the manner in which parents and children actually behave where giving orders and responding to them is involved. This norm and this social relationship form only a small part of the social roles of parents and children.

Social Act • A social act is an extremely small unit of behavior which conveys meaning between two or more persons, a conception of the term consistent with the ideas of Mead and other writers.[15] Imagine two men being introduced to each other by a third who knows them both. One man holds his right hand out in the direction of the other. This becomes a social act when the second man correctly interprets its meaning by extending his own hand. Social acts are the smallest units of sociology proper. A single social relationship may include a large number of social acts. Since sociologists assume the interdependence of all social behavior up to and including the level called society, social acts may be seen as elemental entities to which all other units may be reduced or upon which all other units are ultimately built, however one chooses to look at it. Descending a hierarchy of sizes and complexity in organized social behavior we can go no further than this. "Below" this level we leave the sociological frame of reference and enter that of psychology.

Our list of the units studied by sociology has its limitations. It is far from exhaustive. It does not elaborate on what scholars have meant by the various terms nor report the extensive sub-classifications of the different kinds of units as they exist in the sociological literature. It ignores definitional ambiguities and disagreements. Given present objectives, though, it does convey fairly well some idea of the kinds of entities sociologists have in

[15] G. H. Mead, *Mind, Self and Society*, Edited by C. W. Morris. Chicago: University of Chicago Press, 1934.

mind when they think of social behavior as constituting organized systems. Most of the items are familiar enough to laymen. It is really the special approach of the sociologist to these everyday phenomena which distinguishes his interest from that of other people.

An important characteristic of the list which may not be self-evident is the abstract nature of the units to the sociological eye. Without his giving special thought to the matter, "society" for the layman may simply be a synonym for "United States." To the sociologist it is a class of social systems, defined by the possession of common attributes. A particular society, say, France, is an empirical manifestation of an abstractly conceived class of similar entities. The same applies to the other units on the list.

Since the names given to most of these units are used in popular speech it is also worth pointing out that their meaning is typically ambiguous, more so than most users of the terms realize. Ambiguity and disagreement too may be found in sociological usages of the same words, but scholars are powerfully constrained to be as precise as possible, even when this leads to definitions which "somehow don't seem right" to nonsociologists.

Aspects of Organization
Studied by Sociology

Here we identify characteristics or properties of the units named above. We ask: what is it about these sociological entities that is subjected to analysis? The list following is not complete but does include a sizeable proportion of the more important characteristics that have interested scholars in this field.

Culture and Social Action • In this and the next item we are concerned not only with aspects of organization but also with specialized perspectives of the sociologist in viewing his subject matter. Since both received comment in Chapter One they are mentioned here only to locate them in this overview.

A constant theme in sociology is the distinction between culture and the related body of actual social behavior. Regardless of the unit he is studying a sociologist often makes an explicit distinction between a set of shared ideas about what behavior is appropriate in a given setting (culture) and the overt performance that actually is present (social behavior itself). To take a simple case, a student organization may be visualized either as a system of formal and informal rules defining the proper behavior of its members *or* as a set of interdependent events linking the behavior of a number of people (or both).

In a way, this dualism of viewpoint represents the sociologist's recognition of the universal distinction between the real and the ideal in human life. But the importance of the distinction is due to his assumption that culture and social action are in a complex state of interdependence, that each may be said to be in part a function of the other, so that neither can be understood without considering the other.

Structure and Process • All social life has in varying degrees the attributes of persistence and change. Inevitably, then, sociology faces the questions of (1) how social behavior is organized at a given point in time, and (2) how it both persists and alters through time. The amount of attention given to these two perspectives may vary a good deal, but the discipline as a whole cannot escape a fundamental concern with both. After all, what sociologists mean by organization and structure can only be evidenced through the passage of time wherein orderliness and predictability become manifest. And on the other hand, if there were only change and flux in human affairs there would be no structure at all. Still, we do find that some sociologists are more concerned with the delineation of social structure while others pay more attention to the processes whereby structures are brought into existence, maintained, and changed.[16] The distinctions between culture and social action and between structure and process should be seen as entering into the study of all the remaining aspects of social organization on this list.

Differentiation • According to one broad definition this term "refers to any differences between individuals, social positions, or groups, which evolve in the process of social interaction."[17] Svalastoga goes on to note four major forms of differentiation:

[16] Until recently American sociology has been more preoccupied with structural analysis than with change. There are signs that this is undergoing correction.

[17] K. Svalastoga, "Social Differentiation," *Handbook of Modern Sociology,* (R. E. L. Faris, Ed.). Chicago: Rand McNally, 1964, p. 530.

Functional differentiation, or division of labor, exists to the extent that people perform different jobs. Rank differentiation exists to the extent that whatever is scarce and desired is differentially distributed. Custom differentiation exists to the extent that the rules for proper behavior in given situations differ. Competitive differentiation may finally be said to exist to the extent that the success of one individual or group implies the failure of others.[18]

The study of differentiation is concerned with the organization of differentiated systems and the processes whereby they arise and change over time. Two very different illustrations would be the study of the highly differentiated state of religious organization in the United States and the study of the evolution of different social roles in a small, face-to-face group.

Stratification • When the differentiated parts of a social system are seen as being so arranged that they are unequal in worth or importance or "rank," we are speaking of a system of stratification. By the definition of differentiation used here, stratification is only one variety of differentiation. Although it is somewhat illogical to list it separately, this is done because of the enormous importance sociologists have accorded this characteristic of organization and the great amount of attention it has received from them. In American society the social class system is the most important manifestation of stratification, but some form of stratification can be found in virtually all kinds of social organizations, irrespective of size, duration, or complexity.

The Formality-Informality Dimension • We may roughly specify what is meant here by saying that an organization is formal to the degree that the relationships among members are governed by rationally developed, explicit rules which take no cognizance of the personal characteristics of members.[19] The less this condition holds, the more informal is the organization. While sociologists sometimes appear to deal with formal and informal organization as though the two concepts were mutually exclusive, social structures are accurately viewed as varying in the degree to

[18] *Ibid.*, p. 530.
[19] W. R. Scott, "Theory of Organizations," in R. E. L. Faris, (ed.), *op. cit.*, pp. 485–529. A good though advanced recent summary of important ideas in this area.

which they possess this attribute. A large business corporation is a good example of a highly formal organization, a small group of two or three friends is an illustration of very informal organization.

Conformity and Deviation • Within any social organization there are powerful tendencies (inherent in the nature of the individual member and of social life) tending to produce both uniformity and diversity of behavior. As with the formality-informality dimension we deal here with a continuous variable rather than with two distinct attributes. One does not *either* conform or deviate. Both words may be used, for example, when speaking of the *degree* of correspondence between norms and roles, on one hand, and actual behavior, on the other. Variations in conformity-deviation may have importance for the sociologist in at least the following ways: conformity-deviation of actual behavior from the modal occurrences of actual behavior; conformity-deviation of actual behavior from cultural prescriptions for conduct; and conformity-deviation of one set of cultural prescriptions with respect to another set of cultural prescriptions.

Without some degree of consensus in the cultural prescriptions for behavior and some degree of standardization of people's conduct neither society nor any of its parts would exist. But it is equally axiomatic that social behavior and culture are intrinsically productive of diversity and deviation. The sociologist analyzes the conditions which produce and are consequent upon both of these tendencies.

The Special Sociologies

We have dealt with fundamental subject matter in some of the specific forms used by contemporary sociologists. On the other hand, any single sociologist, especially if engaged in empirical research, always finds himself working in settings which are more specifically located in time, place, and other attributes than the abstract concepts and categories presented thus far. As a case in point, a sociologist might be interested in studying the relationship between conformity of behavior to norms and social ranking in small groups. But research on this abstract problem may be placed in an endless variety of concrete locations: in laboratory groups, in families, work groups, committees, friendship groups, and many others.

Too, through past and present relationships with its environment, sociology is continually pressed to concern itself with concrete, limited social phenomena of interest to society for very practical reasons. As a result this outline of the field's subject matter cannot reasonably be concluded without reference to what are called here the "special sociologies." We have in mind those comparatively specialized areas in which sociologists concentrate upon the study of a single class of sociological units, or a restricted range of the attributes of social organization, or upon a particular social problem. Sometimes the work done is intended solely to contribute to general sociological knowledge. In many cases it may be seen as very relevant for social action programs in the larger community, whether the scholars doing the work had this in mind or not. The number of the special sociologies is legion and constantly growing. This is not surprising, since the special viewpoint of the discipline is potentially applicable to the analysis of any social behavior whatever. Unable to be exhaustive, we content ourselves with some well-known examples.

The "Institutional" Sociologies • As indicated earlier, institutions are a general class of sociological units. Each social institution (which is like all institutions in some respects, different in others) may be made the subject of special study which considers the characteristics setting it off from other units in the larger class. A number of such institutional sociologies are already well under way and others are sure to appear. The sociology of the family is a striking example because it is one of the most highly developed of the special sociologies. Other illustrations are economic sociology, political sociology, sociology of religion, sociology of education, sociology of art, sociology of science, and sociology of recreation.

Sociologies Dealing With Smaller Units Than Institutions • There are many of these. In some ways this group overlaps the previous one, since most lesser organizations can be put within a larger institutional context. Nevertheless, some examples are listed separately because scholars have concentrated on them to a considerable extent, and in doing so have made units smaller than the institution central to their analyses. For instance, one may speak of a sociology of the nuclear family as distinguished from the family institution. In the sphere of economic behavior there are the well-developed specialties of industrial sociology and the sociology of occupations. In the political area we have extensive studies of public opinion and voting behavior. It is possible to speak of sociologies of social movements, primary groups, complex organizations, medicine, and many, many others. There is a bewildering variety to subinstitutional organization in this country and, potentially at least, a very large number of special sociologies dealing in a focused manner with particular organizational forms.

The Sociologies of Deviance and "Pathology" • Deviance is an inherent characteristic of social life, as already noted. Sociologists have long engaged in the study of several significant forms of deviance. Criminology is a time-honored case in point. Other examples are suicide, mental illness, alcoholic and drug addiction, and sexual deviance; the list could be considerably extended.[20] Other disciplinary specialists also work in most of these areas, of course. Sociology's contribution naturally lies in the study of sociocultural causes of behavior ordinarily regarded as pathological or morally unacceptable by most people. The discipline has been so closely identified with the study of some of these problems that the public has almost come to identify the sociologist as a man whose main concern is bizarre or undesirable behavior, a misconception this discussion seeks to correct.

The Sociology of Ethnic and Racial Minorities • This perhaps could be squeezed into one of the foregoing categories, but it has received so much attention from sociologists that it merits separate listing. It prominence is related to the peculiarly important part which such minorities have played in the history of the United States. At any rate the study of such groups remains an important specialty within the larger discipline.

The Sociology of Communities • As one of the important units of

[20] A stunning example of how the study of a very specific problem can both illuminate understanding of the problem and contribute to the growth of general sociology is the brilliant work done long ago by the great French sociologist, Émile Durkheim. See E. Durkheim, *Suicide*, translated by J. A. Spaulding and G. Simpson. Glencoe, Ill.: Free Press, 1951.

sociological analysis the community has become the focus of three special sociologies: urban sociology, rural sociology, and ecology. There is even a distinct Rural Sociological Society in this area. The first two specialties are easily enough grasped; ecology may be more unfamiliar. Taking its impetus from the earlier development of plant and animal ecology in the biological sciences, "Human ecology . . . fastens its attention upon the human interdependences that develop in the action and reaction of a population to its habitat." [21] This approach is not restricted to any particular type of community, it crosses the boundary lines of urban and rural sociology.

Demography • Sociologists are by no means the only scientists engaged in the study of population phenomena, but they have made major contributions to it for a long period. Most college level instruction in the subject is located in departments of sociology. This is another field which was not firmly secured by an older discipline in the early days of sociology, and sociologists soon entrenched themselves. As things turned out, it was to be an immensely important study, since by now nearly everyone realizes that some of the world's most serious problems lie here. In general, demography is the study of population size, characteristics, distribution, and of changes in these attributes.

Social Psychology

As indicated earlier, social psychology is a hybrid social science influenced in particular by the perspectives of sociology and psychology. The orientation of social psychology toward behavior is familiar to every sociologist whether or not he works within it himself. For this reason even so brief a review of sociology's subject matter as this ought to refer to some areas in social psychology of special interest to sociologists. Space does not permit doing justice to a sprawling, complex, furiously growing field.

Socialization • Seen in the time dimension, socialization is the intricate process whereby new group members are taught and learn the behavior, feelings, and viewpoints regarded as appropriate. Its most important manifestation occurs as the newborn infant travels

[21] A. Hawley, *Human Ecology*. New York: Ronald Press, 1950, p. 72.

the long road to full humanity in society, but the term also applies to any situation in which neophytes are entering a social system.

Symbolic Behavior • Many "sociological" social psychologists have laid great stress on the importance of symbolic behavior in the transactions between the individual and the group and the resultant formation of both psychological and social structures. The individual is seen as entering society by the acquisition of language and subsidiary symbol systems. Symbol systems themselves are social, but not until the individual has made them his own can he share a world of common meanings and effectively satisfy his own wants while fulfilling the demands of society.

Social Roles • Roles are often treated as sociological entities— parts of social systems — as we earlier noted. They may also be treated in a more psychological context. For example, the role of child is socially defined and, as a portion of a social system, exists in the behavior and behavior prescriptions shared in a particular nuclear family or throughout an entire society. But for each individual child the role has its "internal" aspects. *His* perceptions of his role may or may not coincide with the social definition. *His* abilities to carry out behavior prescribed for him by others may or may not be adequate. A closely related concept, sometimes called "role-taking," sometimes "empathy," refers to the individual's capacity to project himself symbolically into the roles of others as a basis for his own appropriate response. Individuals differ widely in this capacity.

The Self • The person's own conception of who and what he is has been given serious study by social psychologists. The self is seen as a gradually developing but ultimately quite stable precipitate in the individual of long experience with relating to other people in situations defined by social roles.

Attitudes and Motives • The social psychological study of attitudes appears to have lost some of its earlier impetus. In the meantime, the research literature in this field has become sizeable. Attitudes are learned responses and most are clearly referable to social and cultural origins. Motives are ordinarily seen as more closely connected with basic organic drives, although they too are learned. The study of attitudes clearly belongs in social psychology, but the study of motives, while social psychological in part, verges into physiological psychology.

Social Factors in Perception • Despite the organic basis of perception, the study of perceptual activity in humans involves social psychology because of the overwhelming evidence collected in recent decades that what people actually perceive is greatly modified by their social experience.

The Individual and the Group • The group, of course, may be studied entirely within the sociological perspective and the individual may be analyzed in a manner which takes no specific cognizance of the group. But it is obvious that in ordinary experience the two levels of human conduct are inextricably intertwined. So it is not surprising to find that one of the major concerns of social psychology is the study of their interdependence. Perhaps the two basic issues here are the effects upon the individual of immersion in the group, and the effects upon the group of the peculiar psychological properties of its members.

At this point we have concluded our short journey over the terrain of sociological and social psychological subject matter. Anyone who maps such a trip remains dissatisfied with the route taken. Despite considerable agreement among sociologists on the general nature of their subject matter, the particular manner of describing it in detail is by no means settled. Alternative terms are available for designating the same or overlapping areas of study. There is some tendency for labels to be in vogue for a while, then to be replaced by newer ones. New specialties are rapidly differentiated and given names, while others may cease to attract significant attention. Our description makes no effort to indicate the comparative investments being made today in the different parts of the discipline, and there are great differences here as well as frequent shifts in the allocation of the available resources. Although this list by no means identifies all the specialized compartments of sociological study, it is a blueprint for investigation which could easily absorb the time of far more sociologists than exist today.

Some of the perplexities involved in describing the field's content were illustrated in 1964 when sociologists were for the first time included in the National Register of Scientific and Technical

Personnel maintained by the National Science Foundation. An account of the development of the required list of sociological specialties is given by Hopper in *The American Sociologist*.[22] Because of the nature of the Register quite explicit judgments had to be made, however arbitrary, and this gave rise to a description of the field's content which probably would not completely satisfy any sociologist. On the other hand, it is almost certainly impossible to construct a list that would be regarded by all sociologists as satisfactory.

Taxonomic absurdities can arise at those points at which the boundary lines of disciplines touch and become blurred. A striking example is the classification of social psychologists in the Register. Since psychology happened to enter the Register slightly earlier than did sociology, social psychology was listed as a part of that discipline, with the result that sociologists who report a major competence in social psychology are listed in the psychology portion of the Register. Yet, as Hopper reports, "There are 892 social psychologists . . . in the psychology section of the 1964 Register . . . 355, or 40 per cent, regard themselves as sociologists and 527, or 59 per cent, consider themselves to be psychologists." [23]

SOCIOLOGY AND SOCIAL WORK

Since the subject matter of sociology has just been discussed, this seems an appropriate place to comment on the relationship between sociology and social work. Every sociologist frequently encounters persons who thoroughly confuse the central tasks of these two fields. By now the reader will know that the first and foremost commitment of sociology is to the development of knowledge about social behavior. Social work, on the other hand, makes its major commitment to the application of knowledge. It is above all concerned with the improvement of the quality of human life. Social work is what is sometimes called an "applied

[22] J. A. Hopper, "Sociologists in the 1964 Register of Scientific and Technical Personnel," *The American Sociologist*, 1, 1966, pp. 71–78.
[23] *Ibid.*, p. 73.

profession," in which respect it can very well be compared with medical practice. In both fields there is reliance upon knowledge coming from several scientific disciplines, but the central purpose of each is to make direct, practical application of such knowledge through the use of specific professional skills.

The long-standing tendency of laymen to equate sociology and social work may be due partly to the fact that the two fields share some of their historical roots. Today, however, they have evolved into quite different fields. Oddly enough, it is probably true that social work has been more influenced by psychoanalytic psychology than by sociology, although the latter's influence has been growing recently.

Social work and sociology are not competing or hostile fields; far from it. They are different. Their basic tasks are different; so are the means by which one is trained to enter them, and once in them people hold jobs that are very different in character and probably call for quite different kinds of persons. Sociology is one of several fields which does research of potential utility for the social worker. Social work is one of many areas in which the sociologist can find opportunities for carrying out sociological research.

III

BASIC AND APPLIED SOCIOLOGY

Chapter 1 treated the specialized orientation of the sociologist toward human behavior, while Chapter 2 sought to clarify sociology's subject matter. We now should discuss theory and research, and the crucial interdependence between these two forms of activity which obtains in scientific work.

BASIC SOCIOLOGY: THEORY AND RESEARCH

The term "basic sociology" is applied here to the growing body of knowledge about behavior (ultimately crystallized as theory) and the procedures for its accumulation. The first part of this chapter accordingly deals with theory and research in general terms. Our goal is to grasp something of their meaning in building a scientific discipline rather than to convey the content of sociological theory or describe the methods of research.[1] Later, we shall examine the possibility that sociological knowledge may be usefully employed to help solve social problems.

[1] A more concrete description of some aspects of research in sociology is presented in the latter part of Chapter 6.

Theory and Reality

It is unfortunate that in popular speech the word "theory" suggests to so many something that is fuzzy, naïve, or impractical. Actually, everyone informally "theorizes" a good deal as he goes along in life, in the sense that he applies *generalizations* about experience to specific instances of it. Human existence would be quite impossible if we had to treat each new event as unique. Consider a simple illustration. We overhear a friend say, "If you are friendly to people they will generally be friendly to you." Such a statement does not describe any particular experience. It is a generalization which presumably has been abstracted by its author from repeated direct observations of experience. In its informal way it is a theoretical statement. Notice too that it may be very useful as a guide in an indefinite number of future concrete interpersonal situations, for it is, in effect, a prediction that a particular kind of behavior can be elicited at will, given the proper conditions.

There is really a good deal of similarity in one fundamental respect between such everyday theorizing and the theories we encounter in scientific work, including sociology. In both cases, theories are "maps" or guides to reality, intimately related to close observations of actual events. Folklore and common sense embody a great deal of informal theory intended to serve as a practical guide to experience. In somewhat the same fashion the more systematic theories of a scientific discipline are the best description it can give of that part of the natural world which is its field of study, although in science the primary end sought is understanding rather than immediate application to experience.

It should be clear that both in popular theorizing and in science theories are indispensable and immensely practical because they enable the mind of man to come into workable relationships with a "reality" which is inconceivably vast and complex. The heart of a science is an ever-changing and growing set of theories together with the rules and methods for gathering and analyzing factual evidence by which the theories are constructed. Sociology's *most important goal*, then, is the building of ever more powerful theories for understanding human social behavior.

The most significant things sociologists know are expressed in theories, not in the billions of discrete social facts to which the theories are related. For instance, most people are aware, along with sociologists, that Negroes have suffered from systematic discrimination in this country. To point to this *fact* is not a very significant sociological achievement. Much more fundamentally, the sociologist seeks understanding of the combinations of specific conditions under which discrimination against minority groups does (and does not) occur. By relating the fact to a more generalized, theoretical picture of the ways in which social behavior is organized the sociologist achieves a deeper level of understanding and, incidentally, holds forth the possibility of more effectively reducing discriminatory behavior.

Everyone knows countless social facts. The sociologist knows them too; furthermore, he goes to great pains to discover new ones and to find out whether or not some things commonly assumed to be facts really are such. But he is not interested in collecting facts as the squirrel lays up acorns against the winter. His real objective is to be able to understand the facts, to stand back from them far enough to "see what they mean." Understanding, for him, is the discovery of orderly occurrences and arrangements of social facts and the search for general principles behind such regularities.

The sociologist is no more able to come to terms directly with all possible social facts than the physicist is able to measure at first hand all existing subatomic particles. In both instances it is necessary to deal with classes of similar occurrences, and to do so with the assumption that, under specified conditions, the phenomena act, respond, behave, take place in orderly and predictable ways. The formulation of these orderly sequences and relationships is the goal of theory in sociology.

Isolated social facts often raise more questions than they answer; their "meanings" are not inherent in them. Say we find that the delinquency rate is twice as high in one section of a city as in another. This is a fact; it arouses but does not satisfy our curiosity as to why it should be so. We encounter some additional facts: there are great differences in the relative frequency of occurrence of schizophrenia, suicide, and broken homes in different parts of the city. Each of these facts also raises but fails to answer the question: why? But we begin to ponder them *in relation to one another*. The first things that occur to us are that all relate to some kind of personal or social breakdown, and that all seem to be unevenly distributed throughout the city.

After a while we may think to get a map of the city and note the high and low rate areas for each of these problem phenomena. At once something very striking becomes evident: the high rate and low rate areas for all the problem behaviors tend to be located in much the same parts of town. It is exciting just to discover this, but soon the old question comes back: why? Why should such seemingly unrelated kinds of behavior show such similarity in the geographical distribution of their incidence? Is it something peculiar about this particular city?

Our curiosity is aroused enough to check the situation in a number of other American cities. Rather amazingly, we find the same kind of distribution in these other communities. Here we have discovered a *recurrent pattern* of facts, and once more, even more insistently comes a question: what lies back of this regularity? Is there, perhaps, something about the way social life is organized in the different sectors of American cities that produces characteristic rates of personal and social disorganization? [2]

Notice that our illustration starts with an isolated fact, takes account of other seemingly isolated facts, then discovers a pattern of geographical association in the physical structure of a city which is much the same for each set of factual data. This is then found to be a recurrent pattern in many cities, and a new level of theoretical insight comes to view in the question: can there be factors common to all these different phenomena which account for (explain) the similar manner in which they are distributed in American cities?

We have begun to move towards theory at the point at which we identify similarities among social facts, and when we discover patterns of association among classes of facts. Our theorizing

[2] We are discussing here an important area in which sociologists have been working for decades to develop theory which will adequately account for facts of this kind. Some partial successes have been achieved, but the factual order involved is tremendously complicated.

moves to a more abstract and advanced level as we begin to investigate systematically the possible existence of background conditions which may account for the observed associations between classes of diverse phenomena.

The larger the number and diversity of facts accounted for in a theoretical scheme, the more abstract is the theory, and in one sense, the further removed from "reality." Even the simplest theoretical operation involves some degree of abstraction, some withdrawal from direct sensory experience, as when we agree to let the word "horse" stand for all possible specific animals having certain characteristics in common. In sociology or any other field, the more abstract and general theory is (assuming that it has been properly tested in research) the more powerful it is because it serves as a useful map of a larger sector of reality.[3]

The Present State
of Theory in Sociology

Sociological theory is not a great, monolithic body of thought organized according to strict logical canons, solidly buttressed at every point with adequate empirical evidence. The facts are very different. Rather than one body of theory there are many theories, whose logical interconnections remain obscure. The word "theory" is typically attached to almost any form of sociological thought about behavior which transcends or abstracts from the behavior itself. What is called theory differs a great deal in comprehensiveness and in logical rigor. Also, theorizing in sociology varies enormously in the extent to which it is tied to careful, step-by-step testing in research operations.

Leaving aside the specific problems forming the content of theory, here are some of the kinds of operations that sociologists may engage in when undertaking theoretical work.[4] They may be developing *general sociological orientations*. These are not

[3] Since an analogy is implied in the use of the word "map" it may be well to point out that a road-map is not a tiny *replica* of a geographical area but a *symbolic representation* of it. If we understand the symbols used in constructing the map we can find our way in the actual territory. Much the same thing is true of a theory.

[4] The following classification was presented by Merton in a well-known analysis. See R. K. Merton, *Social Theory and Social Structure,* rev. ed. Glencoe: Free Press, 1957, pp. 86–101.

formal theoretical systems, but broad points of view based on the assumed importance of one or a few major variables, for instance, the assumption that variations in culture patterns account for a good deal of variation in people's actual behavior. Such broad perspectives may constitute mother lodes from which specific hypotheses or even theories are mined.

A good deal of time is devoted in sociology to the *analysis of concepts*. Concepts are the words adopted to represent selected aspects of empirical reality. They are the basis on which a theory may be constructed. Sociology's fundamental concepts do not yet have standard definitions accepted by all professionals. What is critically important for scientific purposes is that a definition specifies very clearly just what facts the concept represents. Without this, communication is impaired, and any theory using vaguely defined concepts is likely to prove sterile.

Sociologists sometimes develop *post factum interpretations.* These are explanations of factual evidence introduced after the evidence has been collected and examined. This is the reverse of the procedure in which a hypothesis is formulated, then evidence is sought which will test its adequacy. Theory based on post factum interpretations can hardly be regarded as having a very solid empirical foundation. This is because the evidence does not really test the theory; rather, the theory is so constructed as to agree with the evidence. Of course, post factum interpretations may themselves become hypotheses to be tested with fresh factual data.

Many sociologists regard *empirical generalizations* as theory, and such generalizations are extremely common in the field's research literature. They set forth observed regularities in the association of variables. An example: "The rate of schizophrenia is inversely related to social class membership." An isolated generalization of this sort has no self-evident relationship to sociological theory in any more abstract sense of the word, but of course may be of great value in constructing or testing such theory.

A *sociological law* "is a statement of invariance derivable from a theory." [5] Many sociologists would argue that no genuine sociological laws have yet been stated, although there are some near-

⁵ Merton, *op. cit.*, p. 96.

successes. This is to say, in effect, that by the criteria of science the more abstract levels of sociological theory are not greatly advanced as compared with older sciences. Although less so than previously, it is still true in sociology that the more generalized kinds of theory have been insufficiently coordinated with research, and that empirical research has been insufficiently concerned with the theoretical relevance of the work done.

Earlier there was a considerable estrangement between theoretical and empirical work which seems curious to today's sociologist. In that period one tended to become either a theorist or a researcher, not both. The theorist often scorned the "fact-grubbing" researcher and was in turn regarded superciliously as a cloistered intellectual whose ideas had no connection with the real world. Ancient polemics aside, both approaches made indispensable contributions in sociology's infancy and childhood. Today, in personal preference, some sociologists work primarily as theorists or as researchers, but they recognize that the ultimate value of what they do is dependent upon the integration of the two kinds of contribution, by others if not by them. Meanwhile, a growing number of sociologists cannot be clearly classified into one or the other category because their work so clearly exemplifies both.

As sociological scholars have come to understand better the requirements of theory construction in science and have sized up more adequately the immense scope of the task facing their field, the nature of theoretical work has changed a good deal. These days, objectives are usually much more modest than formerly. The term "theories of the middle range" has gained considerable currency and reflects this tendency. Merton, who coined it, has this to say:

> I believe that our major task *today* is to develop special theories applicable to limited ranges of data — theories, for example, of class dynamics, of conflicting group pressures, of the flow of power and the exercise of interpersonal influence — rather than to seek at once the "integrated" conceptual structure adequate to derive all these and other theories.[6]

[6] Merton, *op. cit.*, p. 9.

A very prominent feature of contemporary sociology, then, is a large number of theories with deliberately limited applicability, but susceptible to empirical validation using available resources. Sociologists try to tailor the ambitiousness of theory to the level of adequate testing made possible by current research technology and other disciplinary resources. There is always some danger, of course, that many small theories will be developed in such isolation from one another that the ultimately necessary work of synthesis and generalization will be overlooked. Scholars are aware of the problem, however, and periodic efforts at theoretical synthesis are made and will continue to appear in the future.

The Relationship Between Theory and Research

A good sociological theory is a reliable map to some part of the real social world. Confidence in sociological theories cannot be established by ascertaining whether they appear reasonable and plausible, or whether they accord with time-honored tradition, the judgments of constituted authorities, or with moral precepts. Instead, the crucial check is made when the theory is tested by factual evidence of an appropriate kind. To make this point is to underscore the very fundamental interdependence of theory and research.

The universe of organized human behavior is almost inconceivably vast and complex, and an indefinitely large number of sociological questions could be asked about it. One of the most vital functions of theory for the research sociologist is to give him some sense of direction as he goes forth to explore in this great area of social behavior. The fundamental axioms and propositions he holds concerning the nature of behavior can give rise to specific hypotheses about relationships between factors and variables. The concepts he adopts enable him to discriminate some (among all possible) forms of data. "What specifically do I want to find out" is, rather surprisingly, one of the most difficult questions facing the researcher. Theory, even in quite elementary and undeveloped forms, helps him answer.

The curiosity which takes a researcher into the field often has its source in theory. The sociologist ponders a body of theoretical work. Perhaps he responds to apparent contradictions in it, or omissions of possibly significant variables. In short, because theory is always incomplete it always raises unanswered questions, and the scholar whose interest has been awakened knows that these questions *can only be settled by research.*

The most critical function of research for theory is its role as the arbiter of theory's adequacy. No matter how seductively attractive a theory may be to its author, it will have to go by the board if the factual evidence produced by appropriate research procedures says so. Basic as this point is, the significance of research for theory goes further. Consider this statement: ". . . my specific initial ideas underwent fundamental modification, sometimes beyond recognition, in the course of the research. . . ." [7] It is a comment by a sociologist looking back on a piece of his research on bureaucracy. Another man, reviewing his research experiences with adolescent society, says,

> Thus, my present research is a direct outgrowth of the research that began in the winter of 1954–55 through an interest in political pluralism. That it bears only a faint resemblance to the ideas that formulated that earlier work I take as an example of the impact of research on ideas.[8]

The same note is sounded by a third sociologist whose remarks are part of his reflection on a piece of his survey research:

> It is commonly believed that research technology is a mere servant of substantive or theoretical interests. Actually, research technology makes a direct contribution to the content of the field in the same way that the invention of the microscope or radiotelescope shaped the content of physical science. . . .[9]

These experienced research sociologists are saying that research returns more than a simple yes or no answer to the questions of

[7] P. M. Blau, "The Research Process in the Study of *The Dynamics of Bureaucracy* in P. E. Hammond, Ed., *Sociologists At Work.* New York: Basic Books, 1964, p. 48.
[8] J. S. Coleman, "Research Chronical: *The Adolescent Society,*" in P. E. Hammond, p. 209.
[9] J. A. Davis, "*Great Books and Small Groups:* An Informal History of a National Survey," in P. E. Hammond, pp. 231–32.

a theory's adequacy. The unforeseen problems of translating theoretical ideas into empirical observations, the immediate contact with the behavior under study, the discovery of facts not anticipated in the theory — all may have unexpected consequences for the original theory or lead the investigator in entirely new directions. Even the concrete methods available for collecting and analyzing data have theoretical import in the sense that the state of research technology makes it feasible to develop theory in certain ways while it rules out others for the time being. The advent of computer technology, for instance, permits effective testing of hypotheses concerning large, complex organizations in a way not possible until the last few years.

An Illustration • No single piece of research displays all kinds of interdependence between theory and research as these occur in a whole discipline. Nevertheless, a brief synopsis of part of a small study may give a better understanding of how the two go hand in hand. This particular investigation sought comprehension of the conditions under which the behavior of people in small, problem-solving groups conforms to group members' ideas (role expectations) of what their behavior should be.[10]

This work was related to a long tradition of theory and research which held, in substance, that the way people actually behave in social situations is partially explained by the existence of shared ideas of how they ought to behave, these shared ideas being given such names as "group norms," "group standards," and "role expectations." One difficulty with previous research was the implicit assumption in much of it that group pressures were *uniformly* applied to all members and that members responded uniformly, either conforming to or not conforming to pressures. The theory to which this research was related did not make this assumption, but was somewhat ambiguous on the point. Thus research might be devised which bore more sensitively on the theory.

The investigators proposing the new study reasoned something

[10] R. Videbeck and A. P. Bates, "An Experimental Study of Conformity to Role Expectations," *Sociometry*, 22, 1959, pp. 1–11. Only two of the four hypotheses tested are discussed here. Formal definition of concepts and derivation of hypotheses are omitted in view of the current discussion's purpose.

like this: "Let us assume that all group-related behavior among members of a group has a significant relationship to the ideas they share on what the behavior should be. This is the basic proposition coming out of past work. But it is too simple to suppose that people's behavior will either conform perfectly to role expectations or that it will completely depart from them. The normal state of affairs is surely one in which some members conform more than others, and a single member conforms (or deviates) more at some times than at others. What we need to know is the conditions influencing the degree to which behavior conforms to role expectations. It seems likely that some role expectations affect actual behavior more than others, and may therefore be said to have greater intensity or strength." The researchers decided to concentrate on this variable, realizing that it was not the only one likely to be involved.

From the factors assumed in theoretical discussions to be associated with the strength of group pressures two were selected for this part of the study. The first was the relative importance of different kinds of behavior as seen by group members. This led to the hypothesis that *the more important behavior is felt to be, the more likely it is to occur*. The second factor was the degree of agreement among members on the relative importance of different kinds of behavior. This led to the hypothesis that *any relationship between relative importance of behavior and behavior conformity would be strengthened by an increase in member agreement on the importance of different behaviors*. These ideas, so quickly summarized here, actually grew, little by little, from the study of earlier work and out of long discussions between the two investigators.

The next step was to plan a research setting for testing hypotheses. It seemed desirable to use a number of small groups assembled for the research in order to increase control over variables which might otherwise influence the relationships in the hypotheses. The groups should be of the same size, meet under similar conditions for the same length of time, have the same task, and so on.

Five six-member experimental groups were organized and all were given the following task:

You are to imagine that your group is a committee of civic-minded persons appointed by the mayor and city council to analyze problem areas in the relations between parents and their teenage children, to survey the local resources for helping families deal with these problems, and to evaluate these resources and make suggestions for improving them.[11]

All groups met for a total of sixteen one-hour sessions and at the end each submitted a written group report.

One problem for the researchers was to build a list of different kinds of behavior which typically occur in problem-solving groups. This was done by consulting earlier research and by asking members of actual groups to identify particular kinds of behavior which seemed significant to them in the group setting. The lengthy list obtained was concentrated into ten behavioral categories, each of which named behavior having a particular functional significance for group activity. For example, one category was "to give ideas and facts which bear on the work assigned to the group."[12] These ten kinds of behavior were to be put before group members with requests for various kinds of reactions and evaluations involving such behavior in the experimental groups.

The investigators next designed and built a simple apparatus for making the needed measurements. "This consisted of concave wooden trays, laterally joined together and vertically set on a baseboard with a slight backward tilt."[13] In addition, 100 round wooden chips, one and one-half inch diameter (much like checkers), were made so that they could be stacked in the trays.

Here is what was done to test the first hypothesis. Toward the end of the group sessions each member of a group sat down alone before the apparatus just described. Each of ten vertical trays was labelled with one of the ten kinds of group behavior. The subject was given the 100 chips and asked to distribute them among the ten kinds of behavior in accordance with the relative strength of his opinion that each sort of behavior *ought* to be performed in comparison with the remaining behaviors. The more strongly he felt, the more chips he stacked in the tray

[11] R. Videbeck and A. P. Bates, *op. cit.*, p. 4.
[12] *Ibid.*, p. 5.
[13] R. Videbeck and A. P. Bates, *op. cit.*, p. 5.

labelled with that kind of behavior. This procedure enabled the member's subjective ratings to be converted into numerical values which could easily be combined for all members of a given group.

Then the members were asked to allocate the chips again, this time in accordance with how often each type of behavior *actually took place,* as compared with the other kinds of behavior. The reader can see that the investigators were then able to compare the *frequency of behavior* as seen by the subjects with the relative *importance of the behavior* to the members. Using a standard statistical technique, it was found that in all five groups there was a highly significant relationship between the two sets of measurements. This was interpreted as supporting the first hypothesis.

Turning to the second hypothesis, a simple measure was used which indicated the degree of agreement among members when they independently made their judgments of the comparative importance of the ten kinds of behavior. The ten kinds of behavior were then put into a rank order based on the closeness of agreement among members in rating their comparative importance. The rank order thus derived for each of the five groups was compared with the average frequency of actual performance, again using a standard statistical method for this kind of operation.

The results showed only very weak support for the second hypothesis, results that might quite possibly be due to chance factors. Insofar as this research was concerned, the investigators could not conclude that the effectiveness of role expectations in eliciting specific behavior was modified by an increase in the degree of agreement among members on the importance of different kinds of behavior. At the same time, as the results for the first hypothesis clearly showed, behavior was strongly influenced by the *average* strength of role expectations.

One hypothesis derived from the initial theoretical position was supported, the other was not. The investigators pondered the case of the second hypothesis, trying to come up with clues which might account for the results. It was not possible to analyze the existing evidence in different ways which would yield an unequivocal explanation. Having determined this, the researchers could only speculate about possible explanations. Several interpretations which will not be discussed here were put forward. One was related to the appropriateness of some of the measurement techniques, given the theoretical concepts involved. Two raised specific questions about the theoretical position from which the second hypothesis was derived.

None of these interpretations, of course, could be evaluated without additional research. The points here are that the relationship between a theoretical position and means devised for its test were opened to examination, and that the actual research both supported the original theory in part and called it into question. Further progress would require both a review of the theory and the design of additional research.[14]

THE PRACTICAL USES
OF SOCIOLOGY

At various points in this book the view is expressed that sociology's most important objective is the development of reliable knowledge about human social behavior, not its direct use in the conduct of human affairs. Pushed hard enough and considered out of context, this position may seem to imply a strict "knowledge for knowledge's sake" and "society be damned" attitude which is not intended at all. Consequently, it is time to consider an old and sometimes vexing question in sociology: What is and ought to be the relationship between fundamental sociological knowledge and the practical affairs of society?

A great many early American sociologists were personally interested in social amelioration and reform, and saw the new discipline as a potentially powerful instrument for relieving human suffering and guiding mankind on the way to a better future. Hinkle and Hinkle point to the prevalence of rural and religious

[14] To cite one study so extensively in a brief general discussion is to run the risk of its being interpreted as wholly representative of sociological theory and research, which no single example can be. Neither in the methods used nor in the problem investigated is this study especially typical. What is most characteristic is its account of the sociologist's shuttling back and forth between a guiding theoretical orientation and a set of concrete research operations.

backgrounds and deep concern with ethical issues among prominent sociologists early in this century.[15] A surprising number had in fact begun their careers as Protestant ministers. It has continued to be true that the initial motives of many persons entering the field have been highly idealistic. In each succeeding decade, despite changes in the philosophical and social climates of society, sociology has appealed to those who see hope for the solution of man's problems in the scientific study of man. The profound consequences of applied physical science are visible on every hand, the reasoning goes. Why should not the social sciences serve man as well?

While this thread of optimism (both about man and about sociology's value for human welfare) has been present almost from the beginning of the discipline, beside it has been another theme which holds that sociology should remain aloof from involvement in matters of social policy and from concern with pressing social problems in order to concentrate on its central task. This view has been particularly identified with sociologists who see their field as properly belonging in the family of sciences. They are likely to feel that scientific objectivity is especially hard to achieve when the object of study is human behavior, and that the necessary detachment is jeopardized when sociological work is too directly tied to organizations, programs, or objectives which are not scientific in character.

Some advocates of a detached science, and some enthusiasts of applied sociology, have regarded their two positions as incompatible. Over the years this has produced a flickering and sometimes heated debate within the discipline. The "pure scientists" have occasionally suggested, in effect, that their opponents are muddle-headed "do-gooders" who misunderstand the nature of science and delay the proper development of sociology. The supporters of applied sociology have seemed to feel that the pure scientists take refuge in a misconception of science which is really an escape into preoccupation with trivial sociological problems. As so often happens when issues are drawn in black and white, the passage of time has enabled more and more sociologists to see that the choice thus posed is really a false one. The issue

[15] R. C. Hinkle, Jr., and G. J. Hinkle, *The Development of Modern Sociology.* New York: Random House, 1954, p. 3.

in its older forms, at least, seems almost dead. While real problems remain here, they are now better understood.

Certainly there has been a vigorous renewal of interest in applied sociology amongst many professionals. The establishment of the Society for the Study of Social Problems and its official journal, *Social Problems*, is symptomatic. More recently, the new magazine, *Trans-action*, deliberately designed to convey practically usable social science information to laymen, and the publication of substantial books devoted to applied sociology, give further evidence of the trend.[16] Noteworthy too is the fact that the 1962 meetings of the American Sociological Association featured the theme "the uses of sociology."

Sketched below is an orientation toward this whole matter which would surely be congenial to a great many sociologists today, though not all. We begin with a point that is obvious enough but nevertheless significant: like any other discipline, sociology is supported by society, which pays the salaries of people called "sociologists" and the expenses of their research. Furthermore, the United States is a country in which the immense popular prestige of science is based more on familiarity with its technological applications than on a grasp of its disinterested pursuit of truth. As Young puts it: "The expectation of usefulness dominates the popular view of science in the United States in spite of apparently increasing respect for those who contribute to the store of knowledge of man and nature without immediate concern for utility or for reward." [17]

Given these facts, it seems reasonable to assume that in the long run sociology will be supported in a manner roughly related to society's estimate of its worth. It serves the interests of the field, so to speak, to be of service to society. However, there are dangers here, potentially at least. It is hard for the person paying the piper to resist picking the tune. Yet this is precisely what the situation calls for in some respects. The growth of basic knowl-

[16] *Trans-action* (subtitled Social Science and Society) is published at Washington University, St. Louis. Among the books to which reference is made, see especially A. W. Gouldner and S. M. Miller (eds.), *Applied Sociology, Opportunities and Problems*. New York: Free Press, 1965; and D. M. Valdes and D. G. Dean, *Sociology in Use*. New York: Macmillan, 1965.

[17] D. Young, "Sociology and the Practicing Professions," *American Sociological Review*, 20, 1955, pp. 641–42.

edge in the field, and ultimately its maximum usefulness, depend upon its being developed in an intellectual atmosphere as free as possible of pressures from those with axes to grind.

Social support coupled with a minimum of social interference is fundamental to the development of any science in our society, and the achievement of this condition is indeed potentially precarious and difficult when the science deals with human behavior. Here, every man in the street may feel that his knowledge is comparable in kind and certainly as good as that of the "experts," whose roles are not well understood and therefore may seem threatening. The tensions inherent in the situation make all the more precious such social inventions and traditions as academic freedom and science's rigid insistence on intellectual honesty and impartiality. These must be jealously maintained by the scholars whose work depends upon them. And their long-run *worth to society* must be conveyed to the general public as effectively as possible.

In this era, when much of the financial support for research comes from "ear-marked" funds, i.e., money from government agencies or private groups concerned with the solution of specific problems, sociologists have reason to be concerned that the growth of their field is not unintentionally distorted by those who control funds. We are fortunate in this country that deliberate attempts to muzzle or control the work of scholars are comparatively rare, and that suppliers of research funds show a good deal of understanding of the fact that the labors of scholars require protection from interference.[18]

The question is not really whether sociology should be put to work for practical ends; it concerns the circumstances under which this should be done. Beyond the specification that the development of the field's basic knowledge be kept free from outside intervention, there are at least two ways in which sociology can serve society without endangering its own central mission.

One rather obvious approach is to make existing sociological

[18] In many parts of the world (not all of them behind the Iron Curtain) the situation is not so favorable. For instance, in the summer of 1966 the new president of Argentina ordained that the country's nine national universities submit to control by the government, and followed this by arresting rebellious professors and students. *Newsweek*, August 15, 1966, p. 49.

information available in ways which demonstrate its many potential practical applications. It is not suggested that sociology can solve the world's ills if fully employed to that end. Far from it! Nevertheless, a good many improvements on common-sense and traditional methods for dealing with some social problems lie hidden in the corpus of sociological knowledge. There are several reasons why a larger use of this information is not made. One is the difficulty of translating from the technical language and publications of sociology into forms usable by laymen out on the firing line. An inadequate job is being done here.

Furthermore, the task of gaining acceptance of such material, even when highly appropriate, is not easy. People often are wedded to familiar analyses of their problems and accustomed methods of dealing with them. They are often reluctant to give them up even in the face of incontestible evidence that they do not work well.

With proper safeguards there is no reason why professional sociologists themselves cannot directly participate in the application of their special knowledge. Some do, in fact, but most have not shown a great deal of interest in personally participating in such activity. Many sociological scholars feel, and with good reason, that the possession of basic knowledge alone is not a sufficient preparation for engaging in "social engineering," and are reluctant to acquire the additional preparation needed. Despite all difficulties, the long-run trend is toward greater use of sociology's present stock of knowledge in problem-solving endeavors of many sorts.

A second way in which sociology can and does serve society is through research designed to produce information of practical value in solving some particular problem. Perhaps a church in a changing neighborhood needs help in determining what program changes would enable it to continue serving the surrounding area effectively. Both the content of sociological knowledge and the research techniques and know-how of the sociologist may be immensely helpful in innumerable cases of this kind.

In between research undertaken only for limited practical applications and that intended only to contribute to basic knowledge is a growing body of work attempting from the outset to serve both ends simultaneously. A considerable part of current research in sociology now has this character. For instance, a study of mental hospitals may add to our understanding of what Goffman calls "total institutions," and at the same time reveal aspects of social organization in such hospitals which must be changed if they are to do a better job with their patients.[19] Or, in an industrial setting, studies may throw light on how to help factory workers accept new production methods without cutting productivity (a very practical problem) and at the same time add to basic knowledge about the processes of social change (an area of great importance in sociological theory).

It has frequently been observed that, potentially at least, there is an enriching interdependence between basic and applied sociology. While the basic field contains knowledge that is potentially useful, applied research can be made to contribute to the growth of fundamental knowledge if it is conducted, or subsequently analyzed, with this purpose in mind. Gouldner notes that up to this point, unfortunately, neither of these tasks has been done as well as it might be. Much potentially useful information lies fallow, so to speak, and the large body of applied research is underexploited for its possible contribution to the growth of fundamental sociological knowledge.[20]

A slightly different slant on this whole subject may be obtained by switching from a consideration of the *field* and its practical applications to the question of what responsibilities individual *sociologists* have here. To make our point it is helpful to distinguish among a person's professional role as a sociologist, the other roles he plays, and the motives he has for engaging in any role. If a man or woman is a sociological scientist his or her main job *as such* is the advancement of sociological knowledge. There is a small but growing number of persons trained as sociologists whose main task is the application of sociological knowledge in some class of situations. The two categories are not mutually

[19] E. Goffman, "Characteristics of Total Institutions," in *Symposium on Preventive and Social Psychiatry*. Washington, D.C.: Walter Reed Army Institute of Research, Government Printing Office, 1958.
[20] A. W. Gouldner, "Explorations in Applied Social Science," in A. W. Gouldner and S. M. Miller, *op. cit.*, pp. 5–22.

exclusive. Each of these sociologists may at times contribute to both scientific knowledge and problem solution.

If such statements seem very pat, it may be pointed out that potential problems do lurk here. For the "applied" sociologist in particular but also for the "basic" sociologist questions such as this may legitimately be asked: does the person have any ethical responsibility for the uses made of his professional knowledge? Much scientific information can be made to serve both "good" and "bad" causes, ethically considered. Should the sociologist, *as such*, concern himself with such issues? May he legitimately place his services at the disposal of *anyone*, for *any purpose*? When translated from this abstract level into actual circumstances this can be a difficult question, and all sociologists would not agree on their answers in a given case. To raise such a question leads to a consideration of the sociologist in his non-professional roles.

Being a sociologist (or any other kind of professional) is, after all, not the whole of life. No person is contained completely in his occupational role. Sociologists are also citizens, parents, members of churches, and so on. As psychological entities, people cannot be divided into mutually exclusive compartments coterminous with their several social roles. Furthermore, there is a "strain toward consistency" in the person. Thus, to return to the problem in the last paragraph, it is certain that many sociologists would place definite limitations on the social purposes to which they would lend their professional talents, because for ethical reasons arising, say, in their roles as citizens, some purposes would be morally unacceptable to them.

We are making two related points. The first is that nothing in a person's nonprofessional life should make it impossible for him to meet the standards of good sociological work. The second is that nothing in his professional sphere should violate important norms of conduct which have their source in other areas of his personal life. No doubt there are occasions when sociologists do feel that a conflict is present and a difficult choice is confronted. For most sociologists most of the time, we feel sure, there is nothing morally or otherwise seriously incompatible between the professional and other compartments of their lives. Conflicts that do rise can usually be resolved in ways which permit maintenance of personal integrity. If there are cases in which these generalizations do not apply there is of course a serious question as to whether the person should be in the field of sociology at all.

At the beginning of this section it was stated that many people are drawn into sociology for idealistic reasons. What about the motives of sociologists? In one particular sense, the motives which impel scholars to engage in their studies are irrelevant. What is important is that their work meets the intellectual and ethical standards of the discipline. Many motives (some good, some ignoble) may lead different men to engage in the same kind of behavior. One scholar may be sustained by a vision of what research in his field may ultimately do to relieve human suffering. Another may be driven by a consuming and narcissistic ambition. Both may do excellent work, however reluctant the moralist may be to concede the fact.

Still, this writer cannot be altogether satisfied with the foregoing statement. To imagine a situation in which all sociologists were completely devoid of humanitarian impulses is to conceive of a chilling and repugnant state of affairs. It is somehow comforting to know that throughout its history sociology has attracted so many people who are sensitive to human pain and injustice. Better that the field be carried forward by such people than by those who are morally indifferent, even though the task of sociology itself is not to choose among different moral alternatives.

Today, sociology and sociologists are moving out into the arena of practical affairs as never before. In the universities, sociologists are appearing on the staffs of such professional schools as medicine, law, education, nursing, business, and agriculture, where they may participate in training people in these applied fields or engage in research which has direct import for professional practice. In the wider community they may be found doing research or consultation in large corporations, labor unions, prisons and law enforcement agencies, social agencies grappling with the problems of large cities, mental and general hospitals, advertising agencies, the military services, schools, religious denominations, and many, many other settings.

In such places they are engaged in the study of a bewildering variety of very concrete problems, each of which is of intense interest to people who are not themselves sociologists but are enmeshed in problems of their own for which the answers are not obvious. A few examples can only suggest the rich diversity of research which has consequences for action. A study may be concerned with the influence of social class on the treatment of mental illness. Another might deal with the social structure of military aircraft crews. Conflict between labor and management in a manufacturing company is a good example. Other studies can be found of the factors which contribute to good adjustment in aged persons. Sociologists have probed into the special role problems of ministers, and studied the racial integration of public and private housing areas. Interesting researches have been done on the processes by which voters make up their minds in elections, on factors making for success or failure in marriage, and on the effectiveness of correctional programs in the field of crime. Disaster research has yielded valuable information. The list might be extended indefinitely. For each of these examples, several (in some cases many) researches could be cited, in which the findings of the investigators have at least some bearing on the choices problem-solvers must make between alternative solutions.

As sociologists become ever more involved in the affairs of society they inevitably meet many problems. As we have seen, they are quite sensitive to the definition of their own proper relationship to the clients with whom they enter working arrangements of many kinds. They are not always entirely sure what the limitations on their roles should be, and occasionally they encounter misunderstandings of their point of view among those they serve. Still, the general trend is toward a more confident approach to professional relationships with nonsociologists, which itself bespeaks a growth in the discipline's maturity and its public acceptance.

While, by and large, sociology is still underused by the society which supports it, there is also some danger of overselling its potential for problem resolution. If the world must somehow be "saved" in the next generation, it will not be saved by sociology! Sociologists themselves are acutely aware of the limited development of their discipline, but outsiders may have misconceptions which lead them to judge the field on its ability to furnish firm, unequivocal "engineering" answers to questions whose complexity far exceeds sociology's present grasp. Obviously, care must be taken to avoid such misunderstandings as sociologists undertake to serve the community. Yet there can be no question that both society and sociology stand to gain, and increasingly so with time, from the current trend.

IV

THE SOCIAL ORGANIZATION
OF SOCIOLOGY

Sociology is more than a point of view toward a subject matter, more than a body of knowledge undergoing expansion by means generally consistent with the scientific method, and more, finally, than a number of people calling themselves "sociologists." In addition, it is the organizational means sociologists have constructed to serve both the intellectual purposes of the field and the personal-professional interests of the men and women who have found their occupations there.

Like people everywhere who share long-run interests, sociologists have found it advantageous to create organizations which multiply their effectiveness in pursuing personal and common ends. The groups discussed in this chapter grew out of the requirements of the field and its developers, and today are a potent factor influencing the course of events in the discipline. That is why some knowledge of sociology's state of social organization is helpful in understanding the discipline as a whole.

THE AMERICAN
SOCIOLOGICAL ASSOCIATION

By all odds this national association is the most important organization for American sociologists.[1] In 1865 the American Social Science Association came into being, a reflection of growing

[1] The membership of the Association also includes several hundred sociologists from other countries.

interest in the possibilities of social science in a country rapidly undergoing urbanization and industrialization.[2] As things turned out, the American Social Science Association was the ancestor, one or two generations removed, of several more specialized social science societies. One was the American Economic Association, organized in 1884. Twenty-one years later, in 1905, this organization was the immediate parent of the American Sociological Society.[3]

In that first year there were 115 members. After an initial period of quite rapid growth, membership remained fairly constant for a while, reaching 852 in 1919. The next decade saw a swift expansion to a peak of 1812 in 1929, but the following ten-year period witnessed a decline to a low point of 997 in 1939, no doubt reflecting the great depression of the thirties. There was some recovery during the war years so that in 1946 the Association had 1651 members. Then came growth that by past standards was explosive. In 1953 there were 4027 members, and 6345 in 1959. As of May, 1965, the total had climbed to 8892. An extension of the growth rate into 1966 would indicate a good chance of total membership exceeding 10,000. Not all qualified persons belong to the A.S.A. Still, the figures are a reflection of sociology's rapid growth, which seems likely to continue for a good many years to come.

There are four classes of membership in the American Sociological Association: Student, Associate, Active, and Fellow. Student membership is open to both undergraduate and graduate students who are in residence at an institution of higher education and have not yet earned the Ph.D. degree. Modest dues include a subscription to the *American Sociological Review*, a good bargain for persons with a serious interest in the field. Associate membership is open to "Any professionally trained person interested in study, teaching, research or practice in sociology, or in closely related scientific fields. . . ."[4]

[2] A good source of information on the early history of the Association is L. L. Bernard and J. Bernard, *Origins of American Sociology*. New York: Thomas Y. Crowell, 1943.
[3] A few years ago the Society's name was changed to the American Sociological Association. Henceforth, we shall use this name, or the initials A.S.A.
[4] Leaflet published by the American Sociological Association, titled "The American Sociological Association."

The remaining two classes of membership are particularly designed for professional sociologists. Active membership requires a Ph.D. or equivalent professional training, although in a few cases exceptions may be made for persons not technically meeting these requirements. At the end of five years Active members may be eligible to become Fellows. Voting in the A.S.A. is restricted to Active members and Fellows; only Fellows are eligible to hold office. In May, 1965, 24.5 per cent of all members were Fellows, 12.7 per cent were Actives, 30.0 per cent were Associates, and 32.8 per cent were Students.[5]

Formal Organization

The American Sociological Association currently operates under a constitution and by-laws adopted in 1951, to which a few amendments were subsequently made.[6] Officers elected by the membership are President-Elect and First and Second Vice-Presidents. The President-Elect becomes President after serving for one year. Other officers are a Secretary, Executive Officer, and Editor of the *American Sociological Review*. These are elected by the Council for terms which it sets.

The Council is the governing body of the Association. It consists of the officers named above (except the Executive Officer), past presidents for the first three years following terms as President, a representative from each of nine affiliated societies, and a minimum of twelve members elected by the membership. At present there are thirty-two members of the Council. A smaller Executive Committee of the Council holds the powers of the Council when the latter is not in session.

The Executive Officer is the principal paid official of A.S.A. His place of duty is the office of the Association, currently located at 1001 Connecticut Avenue, N.W., Washington, D.C. 20036. Subject to the direction of the Council, the Executive Committee, and the by-laws, he is responsible for the business details of the Association's publications and for other duties as prescribed.

In recent years what are called "Sections" have become a prom-

[5] Based on the Report of the Membership Committee of the A.S.A., *The American Sociologist*, 1, 1965, p. 38.
[6] The constitution and by-laws are printed in *American Sociological Review*, 16, 1951, pp. 386–392.

inent feature of A.S.A.'s organization. These are subsidiary groups of members particularly interested in a limited subject matter area who wish to give organizational expression to their interest. In 1966 there were seven Sections in existence: criminology, family, medical sociology, methodology, population, social psychology, and sociology of education. Each section has its own officers and levies its own dues. However, unlike the regional and affiliated societies, the Sections do not have formal representation on the Council. The Sections have proliferated rapidly, and almost certainly more are on the way. They are the outstanding illustration of the way in which the differentiation of sociological subject matter is reflected in the organization structure of the profession.

As with so many other complex organizations a good deal of the work of the Association goes on in its committees. The various standing and *ad hoc* committees as of 1966 are separately listed below, with brief comments giving some notion of their duties.

Standing Committees of The American Sociological Association: 1966

	Duties
Executive Committee	Implement decisions of Society and Council. Holds powers of Council when latter not in session.
Committee on Budget and Investment	Proposes annual budget to Council; supervises investment and banking activities of the Association.

Standing Committees of The American Sociological Association: 1966 (*Continued*)

	Duties
Classification Committee	Recommends criteria for membership classification to Council; makes decisions on membership eligibility.
Committee on Nominations and Elections	Nominates candidates for elective officers, at-large members of Council, and one annual vacancy on the Committee on Publications.
Committee on Publications	General responsibility for all journals and other publications of the Association.
Membership Committee	Charged with maintaining and increasing Association's membership.
Committee on Training and Professional Standards	Responsibility for reviewing standards for the profession, for professional training and research, and recommending to the Council as appropriate.
MacIver Award Selection Committee	Anually chooses author who has contributed outstandingly to sociology in previous two years; in honor of R. M. MacIver.
Program Committee	Prepares program for ensuing annual meeting of Association.

Ad Hoc Committees of The American Sociological Association: 1966

	Duties
International Cooperation	Responsible for sponsoring or encouraging cooperation with scholars in foreign countries.
International Order	Seeks to identify significant sociological activities in teaching and research relevant to international conflict.
Marriage and Divorce Statistics	Works with states through state representatives to improve the quality of marriage and divorce statistics.
Organizational Relationships	Charged with reviewing the present organization of A.S.A. and recommending changes.
Professional Problems of Industrial and Organizational Sociologists	Appointed to explore the possibility of establishing a Section of the Association in this subject area.
Social Statistics	Represents the Association's interest in improving the quantity, quality, and availability of social statistics.
Sociologists in the Federal Government	Liaison with the federal government, particularly the Civil Service, to advance the interests of sociology and sociologists in federal employment.

Ad Hoc Committees of The American Sociological Association: 1966 (Continued)

	Duties
Sociologists in the National Register	Serves the interests of sociology in adequate representation of sociologists in the National Register of Scientific and Technical Personnel.
Ten-Year Social Science Program for UNESCO	Supports and assists UNESCO's international social science program.
Visiting Scientists Program for Sociology	Arranges visits to smaller campuses by outstanding sociologists (under a grant from the National Science Foundation).
Social Studies Curriculum in American Secondary Schools	Engaged in developing instructional materials in sociology for use in secondary schools, with aid from a federal grant.
Committee to Administer Asia Foundation Grant for Improving Relations with Asian Sociologists	Encourages closer relations between Asian and American sociologists by supplying A.S.A. memberships and publications.

The relatively permanent standing committees will be familiar to most persons with organizational experience. They carry on work necessary to the organization's survival. The list of *ad hoc* committees changes somewhat from year to year, as some finish their tasks and are discharged, while new ones come into existence. They also give more insight into some of the diverse activities and concerns of the Association and changes in these over time.

The existing organizational structure of A.S.A. was approved by the membership in 1951, a not very distant date. Yet for this organization the years have brought great changes which have given rise to considerable strains between organizational form and the objectives of the Association. As this is written, members are giving prolonged and searching consideration to a quite basic reorganization of the formal structure. It is not reviewed here since formal action has not yet been taken, but it is very likely that significant alterations will be made in the near future.[7]

A.S.A.'s Relationships
With Other Organizations

As the largest and most representative body of American sociologists the Association inevitably plays a significant role in maintaining contact with other scientific and scholarly organizations and with other agencies of various kinds where the interests of the field are involved.

Presently, the Association has official representation (varying in kind) to the following eight organizations:

the *American Association for the Advancement of Science*, which represents all scientific fields,
the *American Council of Learned Societies*, devoted to the interests of the humanities and social sciences,
the *National Research Council of the National Academy of Sciences*, concerned particularly with the use of science in the federal establishment,
the *Social Science Research Council*, a private corporation fostering development of all the social sciences,
the *U.S. National Commission for UNESCO*,
the *National Association of Social Workers*,
the *Council of the International Sociological Association*, a world-wide organization of sociologists, and

[7] As this book went to press, members were voting on a new Constitution and By-Laws based on recommendations of the Committee on Organizational Relationships as modified by member suggestions. Developments can be followed in *The American Sociologist*.

the *Board of Sociological Abstracts*, a journal which abstracts scientific writing in sociology and social psychology for the convenience of scholars.

Aside from these regular relationships, the Association makes intermittent contact with numerous other public and private bodies as occasion demands. For instance, a few years ago many state psychological associations began to seek laws in their state legislatures which would set up certification procedures for psychological practice. Psychologists had good professional reasons for seeking such legislative protection, but an unforeseen problem arose in several of the early laws. Without intending to do so, the psychologists had proposed statutes which, strictly enforced, might render it impossible for sociologically trained social psychologists to carry out their studies or engage in any sort of practice. The A.S.A. responded by opening conversations with the American Psychological Association (A.P.A.). While the latter cannot direct state psychological associations, it agreed to attempt to persuade state organizations that state certification legislation should include an exemption clause for sociologically trained social psychologists. The agreement between A.S.A. and A.P.A. further specified that the A.S.A. would develop its own certification procedures for social psychologists in its organization. This has been done through the Section on Social Psychology, and a voluntary certification procedure is open to those who wish to avail themselves of it.

In this way a really vital stake of sociologists in a major sector of their legitimate disciplinary interest was protected from inadvertent and most inappropriate legislative encroachment. Another important example is the continuing Association activities to improve the recognition of sociologists in the federal Civil Service.

Other Aspects of A.S.A.'s Program

There are many more specific activities through which A.S.A. goals are pursued than can be presented here, but two are so important and characteristic that they should be mentioned. One is the sponsorship of scholarly publication of work done by sociologists. Five official journals are currently published by the

Association. The oldest is the *American Sociological Review*. In the latter part of 1965 *The American Sociologist* appeared on the scene. This journal is specialized in the sense that it deals with the problems of the profession rather than the discipline, and it takes over from the *American Sociological Review* the publication of official reports and similar matter. *Sociometry* is another journal belonging to the Association. Its field of specialization is social psychology. The fourth is *Sociology of Education*, a title which adequately describes its focus. Most recently the *Journal of Health and Social Behavior* has been acquired.

No particular logic dictated the growth of this list of publications. The *American Sociological Review*, least specialized of the group, not surprisingly came first. *Sociometry* and *Sociology of Education* originated under other auspices and were taken over by the Association at strategic times in their earlier histories. The same is true of the *Journal of Health and Social Behavior*. Need grew for a journal like *The American Sociologist*, and it was added when resources permitted. Undoubtedly, additional journals will be acquired in the future.

Among other publishing ventures in which A.S.A. is involved, the Bulletin Series on Applications of Sociology is especially interesting. This involves a cooperative arrangement with the Russell Sage Foundation which actually publishes the bulletins. Each authoritatively summarizes the work in sociology which has special significance for some area of application. The five in print deal with the fields of corrections, mental health, education, the military establishment, and public health. Others are in varying states of preparation, and treat business management, law, religion, social work, industrial relations, and police work.

The annual convention of the Association is a high point of organizational activity. Held for several days at the end of August, it is attended by about 2500 sociologists from this country and abroad. Hundreds of scientific papers are read and discussed in sectional meetings. For example, the 1966 convention in Miami presented papers in ninety-one sections covering a vast array of subjects.

During the convention official business meetings are held for the entire society as well as for the Sectional organizations. Many other official and quasi-official groups also arrange to foregather on this occasion. An interesting feature is an employment exchange maintained with cooperation from the professional division of the United States Employment Service.

Attending sociologists make good use of the occasion to arrange countless social and professional contacts with one another. Numerous federal agencies sponsoring research or training grants in sociology send representatives to discuss their programs with interested people. Authors and prospective authors have a good opportunity to talk shop with agents of the many publishing firms who arrange elaborate displays of their products.

In many ways the annual convention is an intense and vital arena for the face-to-face contact of scholars, and is eagerly anticipated by most who have made it part of their professional lives. It is not necessary to be a professional sociologist to attend. Typically, many graduate students are present, but undergraduates too may find the experience very worth trying.

The A.S.A.'s Role as a Professional Society

It is illuminating to view the A.S.A. in a comparative context, for it belongs in a group of quite similar organizations which may be called the learned professional bodies. These have in common their *primary commitment to the advancement of a field of knowledge*. By contrast, another group of professional organizations is *primarily concerned with protecting and developing the quality of highly skilled services their members furnish to the public*. In some instances state legislatures have given such *applied* professions (law and medicine, for instance) virtual monopolies of the services rendered.

The differences in objectives between the two kinds of organizations are not absolute. To illustrate, the American Psychological Association, representing the field of psychological knowledge, is also the professional home of clinical psychology, an applied profession. And, on the other hand, the organizations of primarily applied fields may be seriously interested in the advancement of basic knowledge in disciplines upon which the quality of their services is ultimately dependent.

All professional organizations, whether comprised mainly of scholars or practitioners, reflect the fact that their members make their livings on the basis of their specialized competence. This is why their activities are directed not only toward the advancement of knowledge or the guardianship of professional skills but also toward the occupational welfare of their members. These are not the same objectives even though it can be argued without speciousness that the working conditions of an occupational group and the quality of output are related.

Broadly speaking, it is probably true that the "learned professions" devote relatively more organizational energy to disciplinary goals and less to occupational concerns than do the "applied professions." However, we might recall that many of the learned professions have a very important occupational location in the academic world. Better than two-thirds of all sociologists are so employed. College teaching, of course, is an applied profession, one that cuts across disciplinary boundaries. The profession of college teaching has its own organization, the American Association of University Professors, which concentrates heavily upon the *occupational interests of scholars*. By so doing, it relieves the separate societies representing the learned professions from devoting as much effort to purely occupational matters as would otherwise be necessary.

The specialized subject matter interests and objectives of professional societies are usually so favorably viewed, so uncontroversial in nature, or so far removed from popular knowledge that they seldom arouse public resistance or resentment. After all, who is against the advancement of knowledge, or the provision of the best possible medical or legal services? [8] However, the *occupational* concerns of professional organizations are quite often felt by laymen to be selfish and unreasonable, particularly (though not exclusively) where the cost of the profession to the public is concerned. This source of public resentment is felt most often by the applied professions, although the rapidly rising costs of

[8] It must be conceded that there are exceptions to the point. Social workers, for example, sometimes find that laymen not only misunderstand but also resent good casework practices. The furor aroused by the dental profession's advocacy of fluoridizing community water supplies is another case in point.

academic services may soon make the learned professions more acquainted with such reactions. Where this sort of problem is an old one we find that professional societies are much concerned with the "image" of the field entertained by outsiders.

AFFILIATED AND OTHER SOCIETIES

Nine societies are affiliated with the American Sociological Association, with formal representation on its Council. Seven of the nine are "regional" societies:

District of Columbia Sociological Society
Eastern Sociological Society
Midwest Sociological Society
Ohio Valley Sociological Society
Pacific Sociological Association
Southern Sociological Society
Southwestern Sociological Association

The other two are based on common subject-matter interests: the Rural Sociological Society and the Society for the Study of Social Problems.

Although some of these organizations have been in existence for a good many years all are younger than the A.S.A. All were established independently of the national organization and none are governed by it, although, through Council representation, they do participate in the governing of A.S.A. It is not necessary to belong to the national organization in order to join one of the affiliated societies, nor vice versa.

In many respects the regional societies are smaller versions of the national organization, and the professional interests of their members span the full range of sociological concerns. Members may have some feeling of regional identity but this does not usually extend to the program and activities of the organizations themselves.

The regional societies are naturally much smaller than the A.S.A. At present the largest has slightly more than 800 members. For many, smaller size is one of the chief attractions. This makes it possible for each person to become well acquainted with professionals in his region. Each regional organization has an annual convention organized very much like that of the national society. Aside from the professional stimulation afforded by these two-to-three-day meetings, the informal social contacts and the opportunity to establish friendships and maintain them over the years are among the most valued functions of the conventions.

Since travel time and expense to regional society meetings are generally less than to the national convention these gatherings are especially attractive to students. Both undergraduate and graduate students are welcome, and can find new impetus for their own growing interest in sociology by meeting and hearing well-known scholars in the field.

Three regional societies publish journals in addition to their other activities. *Sociological Quarterly* is produced by the Midwest Sociological Society. *The Pacific Sociological Review* is an organ of the Pacific Sociological Association, and the *Southwestern Social Science Review* is associated with the Southwest Sociological Society.

The A.S.A. and the regional societies are nonspecialized except in rough geographical terms. In this respect they all differ from the Rural Sociological Society and the Society for the Study of Social Problems. Another point of difference is that the latter groups have, by and large, more concern with the application of sociological knowledge to significant social problems than do the others. Both have their own annual meetings and both publish journals. Not surprisingly, *Rural Sociology* is published by the Rural Sociological Society and *Social Problems* by the Society for the Study of Social Problems. The recent rapid growth of sociological manpower would have stimulated the appearance of more such societies based on specialized subject matter if it had not been for the establishment of special Sectional groups of the A.S.A.

There are still other organizations in sociology, although they are not officially affiliated with the A.S.A. State sociological societies have been appearing in many of the more populous states in recent years, and the advantages that go with smaller size may lead to the appearance of more such groups. The American Catholic Sociological Association, with its special interest in the Catholic viewpoint in sociology, should be mentioned. It publishes the *American Catholic Sociological Review*. Alpha Kappa Delta belongs on the list too. It is the national honorary society in sociology, with local chapters at many colleges and universities. AKD also publishes a professional journal, *Sociological Inquiry*.

At this point the formal and clearly visible social organization of sociology begins to ravel out and disappear. Some groups have been omitted but not many that are widely known. Yet the list of formal organizations hardly tells the whole story. Nascent groups are continually appearing and disappearing as sociologists are brought together for long or short periods by common interests and problems. Some of these, far too numerous to mention here, have an impact on the formal organizations.

Overall, the picture is one of rapid growth in size, numbers, differentiation, and complexity. Through their organizations sociologists work hard to keep their discipline and profession viable in this incredibly changing society. They do not all agree as to how this can best be done through organizational means, but most know that organization is essential to their individual and collective purposes, and they are willing to contribute personally to make organization as effective as possible.

V

TRAINING FOR CAREERS IN SOCIOLOGY

Few college students, even those who have given some thought to careers in sociology, have accurate or adequate information about the training needed in this discipline. They have heard little or nothing about sociology in high school, where young people begin to get fairly specific information about *some* job alternatives. On the college campus they take sociology courses primarily for general education, not career preparation. The very youthfulness of sociology as an occupation probably contributes to this state of ignorance. So also does the bewildering variety of occupational choices confronting today's college students. The student hears of many fields unknown to him only a short time before. Sociology is among the less well known.

The number of occupations has grown so radically in recent generations and the difficulty of choosing among them wisely has so greatly increased that the selection of a career has become one of the most characteristic personal dilemmas in an industrial civilization. Despite all the brave efforts such as aptitude tests and counselling programs to cope with the problem, it is nowhere near being solved. Our culture requires each youth (particularly male youth) to *choose* an occupation. Unlike many other societies it does not simply tell him what he will do and then get on with the appropriate training.

So far it has not been possible to convey enough reliable information to young people to insure that they *can* choose confidently and wisely. On the other hand, society's needs for the staffing of its innumerable occupational fields and for utilizing its citizens' potentials are not very well served in the present situation. The poet Gray's line "Full many a flower is born to blush unseen, And waste its sweetness on the desert air" might in this century refer not to "some mute inglorious Milton" living in bucolic isolation but to urbanized thousands frustrated by lives spent in occupations for which they are ill-suited. This writer has never faced a class of seniors in the spring without the feeling that among them may well be a few with exceptionally fine potential for rewarding careers in sociology who have not learned this about themselves and never will.

In this chapter some essential information about sociological training is presented, with informal description and commentary. In the following chapter job possibilities will be discussed.

UNDERGRADUATE INSTRUCTION

At the turn of the century only a handful of colleges and universities offered courses in sociology. Today, the schools which do not have courses at least called "sociology" are few indeed. The field has become a standard part of the curriculum in colleges of arts and sciences, and has proven highly popular with undergraduate students. Among the legions who sample the discipline in one or a few courses, those who choose to major in it are a small minority. It seems logical to view the undergraduate major as the beginning of the road to a career in sociology, and in some ways it is properly so regarded. Yet, as we shall see, the undergraduate major presents some peculiar and persistent problems which somewhat compromise its value as the first step toward a professional career.

It is estimated that 8183 baccalaureate degrees in sociology were awarded in 1961–1962. In that academic year sociology baccalaureates were 15.0 per cent of all those in the social sciences.[1]

[1] A. L. Ferriss, "Sociological Manpower," *American Sociological Review*, 29, 1964, pp. 105–106.

Sociology baccalaureates have remained fairly constant with respect to all bachelor's degrees since 1949, and have declined since 1952 in relation to all social science bachelor's degrees. Sociology degrees have increased in relation to economics and remained fairly constant in relation to anthropology. On the other hand, they have declined since 1952 in relation to political science, geography and history, and since 1957 in relation to psychology.[2]

Ferriss' projections for the future assume a marked rise in the production of sociology baccalaureates. For instance, the estimated number for 1965–1966 is 10,920 and for 1969–1970, 15,100.[3] These figures sketch a quantitative picture of the undergraduate pool from which, presumably, sociology recruits many (though by no means all) persons to replace those leaving the field and to man the certain future expansion.

A study made a few years ago of enrollment in sociology courses adds some interesting information.[4] Its basic data came from the catalogues of 263 randomly selected institutions of higher learning. These catalogues listed 3763 sociology courses, and the problem of classifying them in such a way as to reveal underlying patterns was not simple. The authors used two classification schemes. One led to this summarizing statement:

> "Applications" is the most frequently cited subject matter, closely followed by "Social Problems" and "Social Welfare and Reform"; together they account for 42 per cent of all undergraduate sociology courses. "Anthropology," "Tools of the Trade," "Introductory," "Social Processes and Social Psychology," and "Community and Religional Sociology" follow in that order, comprising 36.7 per cent of the total. "Institutional Sociology" and "Demography and/or Population Problems" trail far behind.[5]

[2] *Ibid.*, pp. 104–105.
[3] *Ibid.*, p. 104.
[4] L. Podell, M. Vogelfanger, and R. Rogers, "Sociology in American Colleges: Fifteen Years Later," *American Sociological Review*, 24, 1959, pp. 87–95.
[5] *Ibid.*, p. 95. Unless one reads the entire article, not all of these categories can be entirely clear. For instance, "Applications" includes courses in such subjects as ethnic relations and problems, industrial-labor relations and problems, marriage and family, and youth. The presence of anthropology here is

The other method of classification revealed that the seven most frequently listed courses (52.3 per cent of the total offerings) were "general sociology, social problems, marriage and the family, social work, criminology, social psychology and anthropology." [6] Social work and anthropology, of course, are not sociology but independent disciplines, each very different from the other, and both different from sociology. When we put these two related findings together (and supplement them with further detail available in the article) this conclusion by the authors is certainly warranted: "With some exceptions, it appears that the further removed is the subject matter from the discipline of sociology, as it is defined in the first chapter of most introductory texts . . . the more courses are offered by departments of sociology." [7]

A problem begins to take shape here. Its character can be more clearly seen by examining some findings from an analysis concerned with the undergraduate preparation desired by graduate departments of sociology.[8] The study obtained information from about nine-tenths of the current graduate programs in the field. Chairmen of these departments were asked to classify various courses on the basis of their importance as prerequisites to graduate study. The author concludes, in part:

> The only courses the graduate departments generally rated "absolutely essential" as preparation for advanced study are Introduction to Sociology, Elementary Statistics, and Methods of Social Research . . . Principles of Sociology and Contemporary Sociological Theory, on the average, fall half-way between the "absolutely essential" rating and "desirable but not absolutely essential." Most of the remaining courses listed were considered "desirable," the highest ratings in this large group going to Development of Sociological Theory, History of Social Thought, Introduction to Social Psychology, and Cultural Anthropology.

accounted for by the rather frequent occurrence of joint anthropology-sociology departments. Despite some ambiguity the statement is clear enough to show its relevance to the point being developed.

[6] *Ibid.*, p. 88.

[7] *Ibid.*, p. 95.

[8] F. J. Davis, "Courses Preferred for Admission to Graduate Departments of Sociology," *American Sociological Review*, 25, 1960, pp. 102–105.

These findings indicate that what graduate departments' most want their students to have studied are good introductory syntheses of the major phases of sociological effort.[9]

Here, then, is the problem. There is so great a dysjunction between sociology as taught to undergraduates, on one hand, and the content of graduate education, on the other, that a major in the field is not really a necessary background for advanced training in a majority of graduate departments. We are told that "Only two-fifths of the chairmen indicated that an undergraduate major in sociology is required for admission to graduate study." [10] This view is widely shared by the staffs of graduate departments throughout the country. Sibley, in a recent study of graduate education in sociology, sums it up:

> A large proportion of graduate students in sociology . . . enter the graduate schools with little specific preparation for what lies ahead. This is true both of the third or more of them who have not majored in the subject as undergraduates and of a great many of those who have done so.[11]

If the reader imagines a graduate instructor in, say, romance languages, or in chemistry, holding views like these he will see the problem in a comparative context.

In order to understand this state of affairs one must grasp the distinction between two different functions of undergraduate teaching in sociology. One is to attract the attention of those who might do well to consider careers in sociology and begin their training. The other is to furnish part of the content of a general education for students majoring in other subjects. Sibley points out that the number of persons graduating with majors in sociology "is over forty times as large as the output of doctor's degrees." [12] And the number of majors in sociology classes is far smaller than the nonmajors. Hence, only a tiny minority of students undertaking instruction in sociology at the undergraduate level have serious, long-run interests in the field. The general

[9] *Ibid.*, p. 105.
[10] *Ibid.*, p. 102.
[11] Elbridge Sibley, *The Education of Sociologists in the United States.* New York: Russell Sage Foundation, 1963, p. 25.
[12] *Ibid.*, p. 23.

education "service" function has engulfed the professional training function. Securely tied to the horns of a dilemma, undergraduate pedagogy nevertheless is oriented more to the visitors in its territory than to those few who may settle down permanently.

Another source of confusion about sociology among undergraduates is the fact that instruction at this level has to a substantial degree (especially in the smaller colleges) undertaken the task of recruiting young people for social work. Now social work, it must be made clear, is a different field altogether. Sociology is a social science. Social work is an applied profession, drawing its intellectual stimulus from a number of disciplines, sociology being only one among these. It has its own nationally distributed graduate training schools, entirely separate from graduate training in sociology. Too, there are far more social workers in the country than sociologists. As a result, many sociology departments are recruiting much more actively for social work than for sociology. Contrary to a view sometimes expressed, a major in sociology is not required for admission to graduate training in social work, although it is entirely acceptable, just as it is not regarded as essential for admission to the majority of graduate programs in sociology.

To seek a way out of the dilemma by abandoning the general education function of sociological teaching would be a serious mistake. In a recent summary of the scientific findings of the behavioral sciences (with particular reference to sociology, psychology, and anthropology) Berelson and Steiner make this statement:

> . . . the behavioral sciences have already made important contributions to our understanding of man and will make many more; . . they are an indispensable approach to that understanding; . . they have already affected man's image of himself, and permanently so; . . they are a major intellectual invention of the twentieth century, and largely an American one.[13]

On the basis of this measured judgment it can be powerfully argued that no man in the middle of this century can claim a

[13] B. Berelson and G. A. Steiner, *Human Behavior, An Inventory of Scientific Findings.* New York: Harcourt, Brace and World, 1964, p. 12.

rounded liberal education who has not some acquaintance with this significant new intellectual resource in his culture.

How well sociological teaching performs its general education function for college students is another matter, and we shall not undertake an extensive analysis of the question here. This writer feels that the single most important objective (for pre-professional and general student alike) is acquisition of the general sociological perspective on human behavior (the subject of Chapter I). It is essential for those who will go on into the field and it is the discipline's most valuable and usable contribution to the more casual student. Next in importance is some familiarity with the major specific theories of sociology in those areas of really central concern in the discipline. On the same level of importance is an introduction to the means by which sociologists, as scientists, carry out research, test theories, and add to the store of knowledge in the field. As any sociologist will recognize, these objectives are highly intertwined. Adequate pursuit of any one of them involves contact with the others.

As things are now organized on virtually every campus, courses which have an immediate appeal to students, e.g., marriage and the family, social problems, criminology, are the ones most likely to be available and taken by students, whether majors or not. It would seem more rational and in the long run profitable for specialized courses to be made available only to students already quite well acquainted with the basic discipline of which such courses are fragmented parts. True, the objectives outlined in the preceding paragraph *can* be attained in the present kind of undergraduate program; occasionally they are. But evidence indicates that typically they are not.[14] Actually, if undergraduate sociology were reorganized along the suggested lines the existing conflict between general education and professional recruitment and training should be markedly reduced. Certainly students who went on into sociology would be substantially better prepared for advanced studies than they are today. As Sibley has put it,

> The prospect of better articulation of undergraduate and graduate curricula in sociology for all or most students must

[14] For some of the evidence, see A. P. Bates, "Undergraduate Sociology; A Problem for the Profession," *Sociological Quarterly*, 6, 1965, pp. 21–36.

await wider acceptance of the proposition that an introduction to the scientific study of society is a desirable part of anyone's general education.[15]

Academic institutions are remarkably resistant to change. Yet there are signs of restlessness and occasional innovations which may point the way to a situation in which the two functions of undergraduate teaching in sociology can be performed more efficiently. Many colleges these days are actively seeking closer contacts with graduate departments, for better preparation of their students. We can reasonably expect to see changes in the years just ahead.

This discussion of some of the problems of undergraduate teaching should not blind the reader to what is good in the present situation. Behind the organizational difficulties stand the men and women who do the teaching. Perhaps the reader himself can testify that often it is very good, occasionally superb. Many a professional sociologist can attribute his presence in the field to the excitement engendered by a fine teacher in a freshman or sophomore course. Without question, a half-century of sociological instruction in American colleges and universities has left its mark on the intellectual life of the country. Yet the evolution of both the society and the discipline now calls for reappraisal, for safeguards against over-rigidifying procedures developed in earlier years when circumstances were different, and for creative experimentation.

GRADUATE INSTRUCTION

A Statistical Picture

Serious professional training for sociology begins at the graduate level, with most students initially seeking the M.A. degree regardless of whether this turns out to be the termination of advanced training or a milestone on the road to the Ph.D. Suddenly the legions of students without long-range interest in the field drop away, and the neophyte sociologist finds himself for the

[15] Sibley, op. cit., p. 26.

first time in the company of students all of whom have made a serious personal commitment to the field. In 1959–1960 115 institutions were granting M.A. degrees in sociology, though of course degrees would not be awarded by all of them in any particular year.[16] In 1961–1962, 578 M.A. degrees in sociology were earned, and a careful projection estimated that this number would rise to 940 in 1969–1970.[17]

The attrition characterizing progressively advanced levels of training is shown in the facts concerning Ph.D. degrees. In 1961–1962 only 173 doctorates in sociology were awarded.[18] More than forty times as many baccalaureates in sociology graduated in that year. Ferriss estimated that doctorate production will rise to 320 in 1969–1970.[19] Sociology doctorates are about 9 per cent of all social science doctorates.[20]

In the fall of 1962 there were 3924 resident graduate students of sociology enrolled in American universities, 2060 of them full-time and 1864 part-time.[21] The enrollment trend is upward and is almost sure to continue rising for some years.

In his recent study of graduate education in sociology Sibley found that approximately half the students he interviewed had entered on graduate training right after earning their bachelor's degrees.[22] The median period of time from B.A. to M.A. for his students was 3.7 years. Other data cited by him suggest that the median period from B.A. to Ph.D. is 9.9 years.[23] Most of the social sciences are comparable in the time period required. For sociologists, and probably the other fields as well, these time intervals are somewhat misleading since there is evidence that the 9.9 years includes several years of professional experience which is not part of the formal training.[24] This is very likely to consist of part-time, occasionally even full-time teaching or research assistance.

[16] Ferriss, *op. cit.*, p. 112.
[17] *Ibid.*, p. 104.
[18] *Ibid.*, p. 104.
[19] *Ibid.*, p. 104.
[20] *Ibid.*, pp. 106–107.
[21] *Ibid.*, pp. 106–107.
[22] Sibley, *op. cit.*, pp. 100–101.
[23] *Ibid.*, p. 100.
[24] *Ibid.*, p. 100.

The M.A. Degree

Today there are, roughly, 3500 holders of the M.A. in sociology who do not have Ph.D.'s.[25] There is considerable misunderstanding about the significance of this degree, which is hardly surprising since the picture has been a changing one. For some students it is a kind of trial run for the doctorate, which is the principal objective. In such cases it is not likely to appear later on to have great importance for the individual concerned. There was for a time in recent years some evidence of a national trend toward bypassing the M.A. for students headed for the Ph.D. It appeared that the M.A. might ultimately change its historic functions or even, ultimately, disappear altogether.

For reasons that will become clear, the vitality of the M.A. is now assured for a long time to come. Meanwhile, it continues to have a number of positive values for the student seeking a Ph.D. Occasionally a person is not yet sure of his decision to enter the field and is reluctant to undertake graduate work at an institution other than the one in which he earned his baccalaureate. If his alma mater is a university, he can undertake the experiment at home, so to speak. Should he decide not to go further, he may still have a graduate degree to show for his investment. If he wishes to proceed further he is likely to transfer to another university for his doctoral training.

Another value for the student is the experience gained in preparing the M.A. dissertation usually required. If he is going on, this effort will help prepare him for the more ambitious effort required of doctoral candidates. From the standpoint of the graduate training center the M.A. program has considerable diagnostic value. It helps the graduate staff evaluate the student and decide whether he should be encouraged to go on. If the decision is negative, again the student has a legitimate advanced degree to represent the work he has done.

The significance of the M.A. must also be evaluated in the light of the fact that a majority of those who take it do not, for one reason or another, go on to more advanced training.[26] What about these "terminal" M.A.'s? Has their position in the job

[25] Based on an estimate by Ferriss, *op. cit.*, p. 108.
[26] Sibley, *op. cit.*, pp. 22–23.

market been improved? We will have a good deal more to say about employment for sociologists in the next chapter, but we can certainly indicate at this point that holders of an M.A. have, in fact, greatly improved their position. Very recently, the demand for college teachers has increased to the point at which very satisfactory positions may be obtained and held with the M.A. degree. This factor alone has greatly enhanced the occupational value of the M.A. The degree is also more valuable than the B.A. for a wide variety of nonacademic positions in government and in private agencies and businesses.

The Ph.D. Degree

As the newly-fledged Ph.D. looks back across his years of study he knows he has arrived at the highest level of formal academic training accorded to scholars in our society. His feelings may very well be mixed, for it has not been easy to reach this point. He will know all the rueful academic jokes about his hard-won degree. He will call it his "union card" and otherwise publicly make little of what he has done. But at heart he is likely to feel, though he may not show, a great deal of satisfaction at his accomplishment. For those who know how to recognize them there are clear signs of the individual and collective pride felt by those who have passed through this door. It is hard for those who have not earned Ph.D.'s to appreciate the scorn sometimes felt by those who have for the too-prolific granting of "honorary" doctorates by colleges and universities these days, or for the somewhat related practice of giving academic rank to athletic coaches. Another giveaway is the sensitivity of many Ph.D.'s to the widespread misinformation among laymen which holds that only M.D.'s are "real" doctors. The Ph.D.-holder knows that his degree originated in the medieval universities of Europe and yields nothing to the M.D. in antiquity, authenticity, or depth of learning. Unable to correct popular error, he is likely to engage in a form of reverse snobbery in which he prefers not to be addressed by the title "doctor." It is as though he were saying "That rude fellow the M.D. insists on having the title appended to his name. How coarse! I'd really rather you didn't address me that way."

As things are these days holders of the Ph.D. in sociology (con-

servatively estimated at 3000) will find doors of opportunity opening on every hand.[27] Insofar as formal education is concerned
they are qualified for any kind of career the field affords and soon
find that people are bidding vigorously for their services.

To make a point about these graduate degrees we may ask:
what is a sociologist? There is no official definition, but here is
one for which something can be said, although it is admittedly
arbitrary. A sociologist is a person who holds the M.A. or Ph.D.
degree in sociology, belongs to the American Sociological Association, and makes a major and continuing commitment (not necessarily full-time) to the use of his sociological knowledge. This
may be in teaching, research and writing, in professional consultation, and in other areas besides.

Holders of the baccalaureate in sociology would not qualify by
this definition, for reasons given earlier. A person who does not
belong to the national professional association would not qualify
on the grounds that a professional owes this much to the organization which represents, advances, and protects the interests of his
field. Commitment of time and energy in professional tasks is
part of the definition in order to exclude those who occasionally
lapse in interest and let their degrees become dead letters. To
restrict the term to holders of the Ph.D. would be unrealistic
today. There are probably as many persons who meet the rest of
the definition as there are Ph.D. holders. Thus, the acquisition
of one or both of the two advanced degrees satisfies an important
prerequisite to the *assumption of a new professional identity and
acceptance by other professionals in the field.*

Graduate Institutions

As compared with the situation only a few decades ago, graduate instruction in sociology is now available at universities widely
dispersed throughout the country. Currently, about seventy-nine
offer the M.A. only, and about sixty-eight the M.A. and Ph.D.[28]
It is difficult and expensive to assemble a department competent
to offer doctoral training. Library facilities must be substantially
better than average, teaching loads for faculty must be compara-

[27] Ferriss, *op. cit.,* p. 107.
[28] Sibley, *op. cit.,* pp. 63–64.

tively low, and from a supply that is far too small, men capable of directing advanced training and independent research must be recruited and furnished the necessary support, financial and otherwise. Considerable funds are needed to assist graduate students, nearly all of whom, it may be taken for granted, are poor as church mice. In view of these difficulties the rapid expansion of graduate training capacity in sociology may be interpreted in part as an indicator of the vitality and growth of the discipline.

The largest doctorate degree production is from the University of Chicago and Columbia University, where the average number per year between 1950–1962 was 15.5 and 11.3, respectively.[29] This measure drops sharply to 7.8 per year at Harvard, and then declines very gradually down the total list of degree-granting institutions. Degree production is highly concentrated, though less so than in earlier years. Sibley records that "Three institutions gave about a quarter, nine institutions almost half, and twenty-three institutions gave four-fifths of the doctoral degrees during the period 1950–1960." [30] Universities granting Ph.D.'s also were the source of the majority of the M.A.'s earned.[31] It seems likely that the rapid growth of new programs coupled with demand in the labor market for sociologists will gradually disperse degree production more evenly in the years ahead.

The question of the comparative quality of different graduate training programs is exceedingly difficult to handle objectively. Even if sociologists themselves could agree on the criteria to be applied (and it is doubtful if they could), the subtler aspects of quality evade the crude, indirect measures available. Without question some of the existing programs are marginal by any reasonable standards. Universities are sometimes overanxious to increase the number of doctoral programs offered, and the consequences can be unfortunate. It can safely be assumed that graduate training is of good quality in all the institutions which Sibley calls the "most prestigious." On the other hand, it should be stressed that *excellent training is available in many university*

[29] Ferriss, *op. cit.*, p. 113.
[30] Sibley, *op. cit.*, p. 67.
[31] *Ibid.*, p. 63.

departments which are not on the short list of the "most pres-tigious."

The student contemplating the choice of a graduate depart-ment can often get advice from sociologists on his own campus. Another valuable source of help is the *Guide to Graduate De-partments of Sociology*, published by the American Sociological Association.[32] This useful publication lists graduate departments, their faculties, course offerings, available financial support, and other information. The first edition does not include quite all the existing programs and has a few other minor weaknesses, but nevertheless is a most helpful tool for students who would other-wise find it very difficult to evaluate the many alternatives available. Much of the information in the *Guide* is of a type which tends to get out-of-date rather rapidly, but perhaps new editions will be published at fairly frequent intervals. With this booklet in hand, supplemented by local advice, a student who makes written inquiry at a number of schools which seem appropriate to him will have an excellent chance of choosing wisely. By and large, graduate training facilities in sociology are not overcrowded as yet. A student with a good undergraduate record is quite likely to be admitted at most of the training centers.

Financial Support
for Graduate Students

It is axiomatic that a graduate program cannot be run without financial support for students. The availability of funds as com-pared with the undergraduate level sometimes surprises students who are learning about these matters for the first time. Yet the need for financial support at the graduate level is obvious. Stu-dents are likely to be in their early twenties when they start advanced training, and no longer regarded as dependents by parents who may feel with considerable justification that it is time to lay down the financial burdens of parenthood. A high proportion of graduate students these days are married and many also have children. They are hardly in a position to forego all

[32] Available at $1 from the American Sociological Association, 1001 Connec-ticut Avenue, N.W., Washington, D.C. 20036.

income for an indeterminate number of years. Students' wives often are prepared to hold jobs, it is true, but sometimes they too are engaged in completing their academic training. Where there are young children it is naturally difficult for the mother to hold down a job substantial enough to support the family while her husband goes to school. In short, graduate students are practically all "needy" cases.

Universities have made a virtue of necessity. Large numbers of graduate students are employed as part-time teachers and as research assistants. "Teaching assistants," as they are usually called, have become a familiar and apparently indispensable part of the teaching force in large universities. They are sometimes used for paper grading and other routine instructional chores. More typically, perhaps, they are in charge of "discussion sections" of large introductory courses. Sometimes, advanced graduate students even handle courses through the sophomore level completely on their own. The rapid growth of large universities, the increase in class size, and difficulties in conventional staffing have all contributed to the spread of this kind of instruction. The teaching assistantship is still, by and large, the backbone of the financial support structure for graduate students. *The Guide to Graduate Departments in Sociology* lists a total of 1266 of them, and the number increases considerably each year along with growing enrollments.

The rapid expansion of financial support for sociological research since World War II has made research assistantships more and more common. Sometimes these are supported by regular departmental funds, with assistants assigned to various tasks as needed. More often, the funds come from grants made to individual faculty members or to research institutes in connection with specific research programs. In all cases, the student performs any of a wide variety of research tasks under the supervision of faculty members. He may perhaps do some interviewing, or observation of behavior, or be involved in various aspects of data processing, such as content analysis, coding, or the operation of data processing equipment, which may include electronic computers.

Fellowships are another important class of financial aid for students. They are distinguished from assistantships by virtue of the fact that they do not ordinarily require duties of the holder. Some are supported locally by public funds or by private grants and bequests. The most significant development here is the recent appearance of fellowship programs supported by the federal government. There are a number of these. In some cases awards are made to specific individuals already engaged in graduate training, and the individual must make his own application, setting forth his program in detail. Frequently, however, the federal agency approves a block of fellowships for a university department, and the awards are made by the department to individual students. One of the best known federal programs is that established by the National Defense Education Act of 1958 (as amended and extended since), ordinarily referred to as the NDEA program.

Other important fellowships for which students in sociology are eligible are those of the National Science Foundation and the National Institutes of Health. We shall not deal with procedures for seeking these and other federal assistance for graduate students in greater detail here, since students will ordinarily be awarded such fellowships or encouraged to apply for them by the department in which graduate work is done. Sufficient notice and guidance along these lines will ordinarily be furnished by the staff of the graduate department. The point is that this source of financial assistance has been rapidly expanding. Most universities also have tuition fellowships which do not yield cash stipends but cancel tuition charges (which in some instances can be heavy).

More and more fellowships these days are being financed by privately funded agencies of various sorts, and sociology graduate students are eligible to apply for many of them. A few examples are the fellowships provided by the Social Science Research Council, Resources For the Future, Inc., and The Population Council. A number of national church or welfare bodies support fellowships in areas of concern to them. Often, these privately financed fellowships require that a specific dissertation proposal be submitted as part of the application, or that a proposal be submitted in a certain problem area. Once again, no detailed information on such programs is required here, since this information becomes available to students after matriculation in a graduate program.

The last source of financial support to be mentioned is the program initiated under the Economic Opportunity Act of 1964, usually referred to as the "anti-poverty" program. This very broad legislation includes provisions for employing college students who need assistance (the so-called "work-study" program), and it appears that this may rather quickly become a noticeable source of funds for graduate students. Of course, a measure of financial need is built into this program, whereas evidence of need is seldom required in the kinds of assistance discussed earlier. Students are paid on an hourly basis.

It is difficult to assess the comparative financial value of assistantships at different universities. The flyers sent out by the universities describing their assistance programs can be (unintentionally) quite misleading. For instance, some universities require students to pay tuition out of the cash stipends attached to assistantships, while others remit tuition fees in addition to the cash stipend. This confusion is made more significant by the great differences in tuition charges among universities. These may range from nothing at all for state residents (in several state universities) to $2,000 or more for an academic year. In addition, there are real differences in the amount of work required of assistants paid approximately the same amount of money, and this can affect the rate at which the student progresses toward his degree. Some schools have different rates of pay for assistants, with first-year appointees receiving lower stipends. Finally, there is an upward pressure on remuneration and any list of the amounts currently paid becomes obsolete fairly rapidly. Detailed information on these matters is given in the *Guide to Graduate Departments of Sociology*. A very rough approximation of the situation can be conveyed by suggesting that about $2,000 or $2,200 plus tuition fees is currently typical, in return for which the student will be asked for about twenty hours of work per week. This does not mean that he will teach twenty hours of classes, of course. His work load will include reasonable estimates of time required for preparation and other tasks done outside the classroom.

Many fellowships, especially those supported by the new federal programs, pay stipends exceeding those usually available for departmental teaching and research assistantships. For instance, NDEA Fellows receive $2,000 in the first year, $2,200 in the second year, and $2,400 in the third year. These amounts can be supplemented by allowances of $400 for each of the recipient's dependents. Much the same situation is true for National Science Foundation Fellows. They receive first-year stipends of $2,400. This rises to $2,600 in the second year and $3,000 in the terminal year. Each dependent adds $500 to the base figure. Fellows in the National Institutes of Health program receive $1,800 initially, followed by $2,000 in the second year, $2,400 in the third year, and $3,000 in the final year. Again $500 dependency allowances are available. All three federal programs pay tuition fees in addition to cash stipends. A fourth-year NIH Fellow, married and with two children, would receive $4,500 at current rates.

What is the import of all this for the student contemplating graduate training? It should be clear that he is in a very favorable position, more so than at any time in the recent past. When it comes to choosing a graduate department of sociology, he has a wide range of choices. He would do well to secure graduate catalogs and departmental bulletins (where available) from all in which he has any interest, and compare them carefully as well as he can with the help of his advisors. It is perfectly legitimate to apply to several schools for admission and for financial support. If his undergraduate record is good (not necessarily at the top by any means), his chances of admission and financial support are excellent.

Usually, the department will assign him a fellowship or assistantship without consulting him. A choice is ordinarily not his at this juncture. Looking at the alternatives from his point of view there are advantages and disadvantages to each. With a fellowship he can carry a heavier academic load and make more rapid progress toward his goal. On the other hand, he misses the opportunity to do some teaching or have some supervised research experience. Many graduate students value such experience very highly, and properly so. It is quite possible, of course, that before he completes his training he will have had an opportunity to hold both fellowships and assistantships, a good combination.

Applications for admission and assistance may be made at any time, but are most appropriately sent in during the late fall and winter preceding the academic year in which the work is to be started. Universities make offers to students in the early spring. Once a student has received and accepted a formal offer of assistance he should not resign from the appointment in order to accept an offer of assistance from another school. This is in accordance with an agreement among the member schools of the Association of American Universities. Compelling personal reasons may, of course, make it necessary for him to withdraw.

The Life of a
Graduate Student

In A *Tale of Two Cities* Dickens wrote:

It was the best of times, it was the worst of times, it was the age of wisdom, it was the age of foolishness, it was the epoch of incredulity, it was the season of Light, it was the season of Darkness, it was the spring of hope, it was the winter of despair, we had everything before us, we had nothing before us. . . .

He spoke of the French Revolution, but his words can introduce some remarks about the experience of graduate training. It is compounded of rewarding and frustrating elements, a time of steadily expanding intellectual horizons but also of confusion and doubt. For most it is an experience that cuts deep and will have consequences spreading out through the rest of life.

We begin with brief references to the content of graduate training, then move to other matters which affect the equilibrium of the graduate student and his ability to keep moving toward his goal. There is both similarity and great variation in the specific content of graduate training in sociology among the many centers where it is offered. Accordingly, it is impossible in so brief a summary to do more than emphasize the similarities of content.

As shown earlier, it must be assumed that students beginning graduate training, regardless of undergraduate background, are poorly informed about the field of sociology. Occasional conspicuous exceptions hardly weaken this generalization. In one way or another, consequently, the first year of the graduate program is likely to be devoted to imparting the fundamentals of the discipline as a platform on which to build more advanced or specialized studies later.

By whatever titles courses are known they are likely to emphasize two principal concerns: "theory" and "research methods." The work in theory is likely to acquaint students with some of the major contributors to sociological thought in the past and some brief introduction to major theoretical orientations in present-day sociology. In methods (which probably includes separate training in statistics) the student will encounter the range of research techniques used by sociologists for collecting data scientifically. In some departments he will also do a modest amount of actual, supervised research.

As time goes on the student will take more advanced courses and seminars, some probing more deeply into the theoretical and methodological fundamentals of the discipline, others much more specialized and concerned with highly divided portions of the field. In some departments he is likely to take a minor in a different field, but the more typical national picture shows that all his work will be done in sociology.

Each doctoral student will need to prepare himself in several basic or specialized areas, typically two to four, in addition to theory and methods. The graduate department defines these for its students. Usually certain fields are required, while others may be elected by the student. Departments vary a great deal in the number of fields of specialization open to their students. For example, one department offers seventeen, and even this number by no means exhausts the variety of specialized studies in today's sociology.[33]

Throughout his graduate training, the student will read, and read, and then read some more. His instructors will expect him to read a great deal for their courses and seminars but he will also be expected to read widely in the discipline on his own. Concurrently with his course work, he is likely to be concerned with the foreign language requirements of his university. As is true in most of the departmental graduate programs in the arts and sciences, students in most cases are required to pass examinations

[33] Sibley, *op. cit.*, p. 122.

of reading knowledge (usually reading examinations) in two foreign languages. A few universities will accept really good performance in one language, and a few others allow the substitution of extra work in some related field for one of the languages. The language requirements are imposed by the graduate schools of the universities and are not directly subject to modification by individual departments.

Somewhere along the line, especially at the doctoral level, the student will become closely associated with a single major advisor and/or supervisory committee. This committee approves the details of his program of studies and particularly supervises his dissertation research. He or it will be directly involved in several of the formal *rites de passage* built into graduate training. Some departments require a qualifying examination at or near the beginning of graduate training. This is likely to have largely diagnostic value, indicating something about the student's potential, more, perhaps, about the work needed. In some departments one or more other examination points will be found in addition to the formal written and oral examinations. The latter are typically given when most or all of the formal course work has been completed, and are broadly based tests of the knowledge required rather than course examinations. Ordinarily, at the very end of the training period there is also a formal oral examination and defense of the dissertation.

The list of institutionalized "gateways" through which the individual must successively pass on his way to a Ph.D. degree, then, looks something like this:

1. Qualifying examination.
2. Passage of reading examinations in two foreign languages.
3. Admission to candidacy.
4. Establishment of supervisory committee.
5. Approval of program.
6. Approval of dissertation plan.
7. Completion of course work.
8. Passage of comprehensive examinations.
9. Completion and acceptance of dissertation.
10. Oral defense of dissertation.

This list is similar to but somewhat longer than that for M.A. students. While most departments require a dissertation of their M.A. students, a minority do not, especially for students who are terminal at the M.A. level. Both at the M.A. and Ph.D. levels, but especially in the latter case, the dissertation is a most important part of the whole program. Sociology is a research field and the neophyte professional is ordinarily expected to demonstrate his capacity to carry out a modest but competently designed research project. Occasionally, theoretical dissertations not involving the collection and analysis of empirical data are also approved. While some degree of supervision and assistance can be expected by the candidate, he must demonstrate sufficient professional maturity to conceive and execute a study largely on his own.

Graduate Training as Metamorphosis

Having considered the content of graduate work, let us look briefly at other aspects of the complex and fascinating process whereby a person becomes a sociologist. We are concerned here with what social psychologists call "adult socialization." At the same time our topic relates to the manner in which a profession recruits and trains personnel in order to insure its continuity and development. What goes on has, so to speak, both "inner" and "outer" significance, and the two aspects subtly and deeply interpenetrate.

The American university today is sufficiently compartmentalized so that persons in one compartment can be remarkably poorly informed about what goes on in the others. In the case under discussion here, undergraduate students typically know much less than they probably realize about the life of the graduate student. The break from undergraduate to graduate training is a sharp one. In many ways the student moves into a new world whose features he knows only dimly, and for which he has consequently been unable to prepare very effectively in advance.

Here are some of the things that are likely to be true of the beginning graduate student in sociology. He has had some undergraduate work in the field, but not enough or of the right kind to give him a very clear picture of the discipline as perceived by the professionals in it. He may see sociology in a rather vague way as being an avenue for the betterment of mankind, a discipline sensitive to the sore spots in civilization and dedicated to alleviating them. This appeals to his idealism, since he is likely to be a person who would want his life in some way to serve the cause of human welfare and progress. The chances are good that he is attracted to the idea of becoming a college teacher and may possibly be as much interested in this kind of work as he is in sociology itself.

Graduate training is seen as a continuation of the student role he has played for so many years. Of course it is, but he does not yet grasp how greatly this role alters at the graduate level. More than he realizes, formal education has been a rather passive process for him up to this point. Even in college he has attended classes with clearly demarcated units of subject matter and fairly clear expectations of what he is to do presented by the professor. He probably has quite deep-seated habits compatible with this rather passive intellectual posture. Is it not so with many undergraduates that one definition of the "good" professor specifies that he gives carefully organized lectures which can easily be committed to the student's notes, and tests whose nature is safely predictable?

The new student is also likely to be somewhat ambivalent about undertaking graduate work, although he may not be aware of it at this point. After all, many of his friends are now moving out into "real" jobs after receiving the baccalaureate degree, finding places in their communities, and establishing their homes. He, on the other hand, must look forward to more years of low income and marginal adulthood. At the same time there may very well be a haunting uncertainty as to whether he is really on the right path, or sufficiently committed to it.

What does the new graduate student meet as he begins his studies? One of the most important, pervasive, and devastating things is the *ambiguity* of the experience. This shows up clearly in the courses he takes. Gone is the familiar textbook with its assignment for next time. Gone is the lecture with its portion of knowledge more or less neatly doled out at each class section.

Most of his courses will have an informality which initially charms, but may come to frighten because the instructor mysteriously refuses to act as instructors have in the past. Little by little it dawns on the student that his professor is not being lazy or perverse, but actually expects him to be a really active partner in a joint venture. He must show initiative, imagination, and a self-starting capacity which perhaps have never been seriously challenged before in an educational context. It is one thing to grasp this intellectually. It is a harder thing to break old habits of passive dependence upon the teacher and build new ones of cooperative study and investigation. In the process the faculty member is the senior partner, but he and the student are nevertheless to be true partners.

Thus, the way in which graduate training is organized contributes something to the ambiguity of the situation. More is added, in sociology, by the very nature of the field. It does not take the student long to realize how little he knows about sociology and social psychology. As he turns with a will to getting really acquainted with the discipline, he discovers something which for some can be quite unsettling. He learns that truth in sociology is provisional and problematic. Consciously or unconsciously, the student probably yearns for simple, clear-cut answers to simple, clear-cut questions. But there aren't any in sociology. The slow realization of this can be a critical point in the student's feeling about his chosen field, since this characteristic is something he must learn to live with permanently.

Most students hold graduate teaching or research assistantships during part or even all of their training. In either case, but particularly where teaching duties are involved, the experience is likely to be important in the process of becoming a professional. Suddenly a person finds himself in front of a classroom of students and experiences for the first time the peculiar polarization of classroom interaction. Now, instead of sitting in the anonymous throng he feels every eye on him, feels the weight of the collective expectancy, neutral at first but so easily transformed into skepticism, even hostility. For the subtle and demanding work of teaching college students he has, like other college instructors, received no real training at all. In time he will get accustomed to all this, but we may well sympathize with him at this moment.

The graduate assistant is a good example of what the sociologist calls the "marginal man." He is both faculty member and student, but not fully one or the other. The roles of teacher and student are defined in terms of each other. While they are by definition complementary, their relationship incorporates some degree of tension and hostility, which can present some adjustment problems for the teaching assistant. To his own students he is teacher (even if they know his true status). To his professors he is student. The situation makes it impossible for him to be quite at home in either world. There are marginal men roles elsewhere in society where the actors are expected to continue indefinitely. Foremen in factories and noncommissioned officers in the military are examples. In such cases the social situation usually mitigates some of the built-in hardships of marginality. This is not so for the graduate assistant, since he is supposed to move on through and out of the social system, to be replaced by others. Hence, the internal conflicts engendered by marginality here probably operate as forces urging the student toward completion of his training and tests of his determination to enter the discipline.

Under the circumstances, the student's relationships with his peers in the same program are ordinarily highly significant, however much they may vary from one time or place to another. Whatever the specific characteristics of informal organization among graduate students, it is almost certain that the individual will seek here for sustaining relationships and experiences. For one thing, he will take pleasure in the simple fact that he is now in the company of others moving in the same direction. As an undergraduate he was likely to feel rather lost in the hordes of students not seriously interested in sociology. Now all his present peers share his interest, thus validating his own decision in a significant and helpful way.

As problems and frustrations occur in the course of his training, he is likely to find sympathy and support from these others who know at first hand what he is experiencing. Cut off from earlier friendships, excluded from full admission into the social world of the faculty, and beyond the pale of undergraduate society, he is likely to find his friendships and his social life among his fellow students. Some of these relationships will last the rest of his life, long after he and his fellows have scattered to the far corners of the country. The early experiences shared in graduate training, the shared interest in the same discipline, and the high degree of communication amongst professionals will make these some of the most important associations he will have from this time on.

At the same time that he seeks (and usually obtains to some extent, at least) support from his fellows, some ambivalence characterizes the relationships here as elsewhere in the world of the graduate student. There is a good deal of competitiveness among graduate students, a good deal of measuring of one's own capacities and growth against that of others. More than one Ph.D. could testify that in the face of discouragement he prevailed because if his friend Bill could make it, then he could too!

In the circumscribed world of graduate training the senior professors are crucially important figures. One's fate is in their hands. The student has made his decision, has committed himself to the task of becoming a professional, and now these few men sit in judgment on his efforts. For each student a great deal is at stake. Small wonder that each professor is scrutinized both as a man and as a professional for information which will aid appropriate response to him. Barriers to full communication created by the often intense teacher-student relationship at the graduate level lead sometimes to the creation of surprisingly distorted images of graduate faculty members among graduate students. A kind of folklore grows up and is perpetuated which, however oversimplified and indeed inaccurate, helps provide some clarity and direction in important relationships in which the student feels comparatively powerless. The same communication barriers also keep faculty members in most cases from being very well informed about some of the less obvious aspects of life among the graduate students. Faculty members, too, have their myths. Of course, it sometimes happens that a particular student or faculty member has unusual facility in breaking through the obstacles to fuller communication. And, too, as the student matures and approaches the end of his training, it is rather typically found that he and his mentors can approach one another on something closer to genuine colleagueship and even friendship.

Little by little as graduate training proceeds, the student acquires a firmer grasp of the discipline he has chosen, and of his place in it. The motives which brought him into the field are likely to evolve into the motives of the professional sociologist. The search for reliable scientific knowledge about human social behavior becomes a meaningful goal. Some parts of the discipline will inevitably interest him more than others, and as he invests in these his fascination with them grows. He will now think more realistically about the career possibilities open to him, weighing full-time research against teaching in four-year colleges where the transmission of sociological knowledge is emphasized, and against positions on university faculties where research and advanced training are added to undergraduate instruction. Now he not only aspires to professional status; he begins to *feel* like a professional. He notices that younger graduate students show a certain deference toward him, and that his mentors seem more fully accepting of him.

At the end, the student reflects the complex interaction between the way in which graduate training is socially structured and what he himself brought to the experience. Serious graduate work in sociology is not easy, as we have suggested. Properly understood and approached, sociology is an intellectually difficult field, and aside from this the organization of graduate training creates some problems for those involved.

Yet it would be unfortunate if this description seems discouraging. Much of what we have said applies equally well to advanced training in any discipline, where men are seeking to reach and push back the limits of human knowledge. There is no way to make such an endeavor easy and painless. At the same time, the challenges and opportunities are unlimited. To counterbalance the long hours of hard study there are the moments of exhilaration as new insights arrive, sometimes with dramatic suddenness, and a whole section of the jigsaw puzzle seems to fall into place. Against the discouragement of occasional failure and the feeling that one will never finish, the student may put the victories, all the sweeter because hard won, and the realization that he is moving forward into a more confident relationship of self to chosen career. Against the interpersonal rivalries and tensions one may count the warm friendships, and the unexpected episodes in which a faculty member reveals his understanding and sympathy.

At the end of his training the young sociologist is too close to the experience to evaluate it objectively. That will come with time and greater experience. But he does know that he has done something very hard and worthwhile. He knows that he has earned his membership in the community of scholars in his discipline, and in doing so has done a lot of growing up. His field of study has now put its stamp on him, but the same process which produced this effect has also made it possible for him to leave his own mark on the discipline. His generation of scholars will not only carry the field forward but will change it before the next generation comes on the scene.

VI

CAREERS IN SOCIOLOGY

The demand for trained sociologists is greater today than at any time in the past. It has outstripped the supply, a condition likely to continue for some years to come. This chapter contains information about demand and supply in the sociological job market and discusses various kinds of employment available in enough detail to furnish some basis for realistic comparison and appraisal.

A Bachelor of Arts degree with a major in sociology does not give the holder entry into professional sociology. Nevertheless, a few comments on the occupational value of undergraduate training will not take us too far afield. Along with all holders of baccalaureates from liberal arts colleges, those in sociology participate in a general improvement of accessibility to many kinds of jobs. Many business firms and government agencies are interested in obtaining the services of well educated young people without regard to their areas of special interest. Such employers typically feel that a good general education makes an excellent foundation for specialized skills, which can be best transmitted by the employing organization.

A slightly more specialized perspective is found among employers who prefer college graduates with majors in the social science area. These are not likely to require a sociology major, but to find it equally acceptable with majors in one or more other fields, such as economics, political science, history, or psychology. So far as the writer knows, *most* of this kind of demand is found in public agencies, rather than in the private sector of the economy. For instance, in many parts of the country, students with undergraduate majors in sociology or one of the other social sciences can often find positions as junior social workers in county welfare departments or occasionally in other public agencies furnishing relief or casework services. At the state or local level, students with sociology majors can also sometimes obtain positions in police departments, probation and parole services, or offices of city planning.

A number of federal agencies employ personnel for positions in which a major in one or another of the social sciences is a desirable background. In the past this was true of several agencies located in the Departments of Agriculture, Commerce, Health, Education and Welfare, and State, and no doubt will be true of agencies in the new Department of Urban Affairs. Local civil service offices as well as college employment services usually have the necessary information on examinations for such positions. Such appointments are at junior professional levels, but make possible lifetime careers in the federal civil service.

It must be understood that almost none of these jobs are strictly sociological in nature. They simply utilize a particular kind of general educational background upon which to build a variety of careers outside the field of sociology proper. That is why they seldom make sociological training an *indispensable* prerequisite. Nevertheless, undergraduate sociology without doubt makes a valuable contribution to these areas of employment.

We turn at this point to our principal concern: the job market for persons who are in fact sociologists.

TYPES OF EMPLOYMENT:
AN OVERVIEW

Some basis for estimating the occupational distribution of sociologists is provided by two studies. One, by Matilda White Riley, is based on the 1950 and 1959 Directories of Members of the American Sociological Association.[1] The other, part of a larger

[1] M. W. Riley, "Membership of the American Sociological Association, 1950–1959," *American Sociological Review*, 25, 1960, pp. 914–926.

study by Elbridge Sibley, uses information from a 25 per cent random sample of persons receiving Ph.D.'s from American institutions, 1936–1959, and from persons having the M.A. but not the Ph.D. degree, and receiving the M.A. at some time between 1953–1958.[2] While similar in many respects, there are also differences between the studies, so that each has something useful to contribute to the present discussion.

We begin with Tables 1 and 2, the first from Riley's article, the second from the Sibley monograph. They deserve careful study because in highly condensed form they reveal considerable information about the occupational distribution of sociologists.

We shall not attempt to interpret these tables exhaustively, but a number of particularly salient points call for comment. In the first place, the predominance of academic employment is very clear. Adding the liberal arts and professional school figures for 1959 in Table 1 gives 70 per cent of the total. According to Table 2, 73 per cent of sociologists with Ph.D.'s were employed by universities and four-year colleges. Note (Table 1) that the proportion of all academically employed sociologists declined only slightly from 1950 to 1959. However, within this proportion there was a somewhat larger decline in the number employed in liberal arts settings and a modest increase in the proportion on the faculties of professional schools. Almost certainly this trend has continued at an accelerated pace in the sixties.

Reflected here is a rapid growth of interest in the sociologist's knowledge of society and his research know-how, coming from other professions (or, perhaps more accurately, from training programs in other professions). Clear signs of this new interest in the sociologist's area of competence have appeared in such diverse fields as medicine, nursing, dentistry, law, education, social work, the ministry, and business administration. And so we find more and more professional schools seeking to add sociologists to their faculties.

[2] E. Sibley, *The Education of Sociologists in the United States.* New York: Russell Sage Foundation, 1963. In Appendix B, p. 188, Sibley indicates that "The sample was drawn from the 1959 directory of members of the American Sociological Association and, for non-members, from the roster of doctoral degrees maintained by the Office of Scientific Personnel, National Research Council." With respect to M.A.'s, Sibley states, p. 189, that "Address lists of their graduates were obtained from 28 institutions which had granted appreciable numbers of master's degrees in the period 1953–1958."

TABLE 1 · Occupational Affiliation*

	1950	1959
	Per Cent	Per Cent
Liberal arts	67	59
Professional school	8	11
Business administration, technology, agriculture	2	3
Education	3	2
Medicine, nursing, dentistry	1	3
Law	**	**
Theology	1	1
Social Work	1	1
Miscellaneous	**	1
Retired	**	**
Federal Government	5	5
Commerce, agriculture	2	1
Corrections	**	**
Education	**	**
Health	1	1
Information	**	**
Justice	**	**
Military	1	2
Welfare	**	1
Miscellaneous	1	*
Other types of affiliation	17	21
Business, industrial	5	6
Correctional	1	1
Educational	1	2
Health	2	3
Informational	1	1
Legal	**	**
Religious	1	1
Welfare	3	3
Miscellaneous	3	3
Retired	**	1
No information	3	4
Total non-student members	100	100
Excluding members giving name and address only	—	—

** Less than .5 per cent.

* From M. W. Riley, "Membership of the American Sociological Association, 1950–1959," *American Sociological Review*, 25, 1960, p. 921.

TABLE 2 · Percentage Distributions of Ph.D.'s and M.A.'s, by Primary Employment*

Employment	Per Cent of Ph.D.'s[a]	Per Cent of M.A.'s[b]		
		"Terminal"	"Nonterminal"	All M.A.'s
On teaching and research staffs of universities and four-year colleges	73	13	62	30
Other teaching and educational service	5	25	6	18
Research in nonacademic positions	12	5	10	7
Health, welfare, religious, correctional work	0	27	10	20
Other consultation and administration in nonacademic positions	2	10	2	8
Employment not classified above	3	8	1	6
Full-time students	—	1	6	3
Not employed	2	10	2	7
Total	100	100	100	100
Number of respondents	357	176	95	271

[a] Figures for Ph.D.'s differ slightly from those in Table 4 because of exclusion of 44 who did not return Schedule II-B.

[b] M.A.'s classified as "nonterminal" are those who state that they expect definitely or probably to take Ph.D. degree in sociology.

Sources: Schedules II-B and V.

* From E. Sibley, *The Education of Sociologists in the United States.* New York: Russell Sage Foundation, 1963, p. 56.

Table 2 reveals the differential significance for employment of the Ph.D. and M.A. degrees. Notice the small proportion of "terminal" M.A.'s on the staffs of universities and four-year colleges as compared with Ph.D.'s and "non-terminal" M.A.'s. Degree-granting institutions very strongly desire to have as many Ph.D.'s as possible on their faculties. Many, especially the four-year colleges, employ staff with only the M.A., however, because the supply of Ph.D.'s is inadequate. In employing M.A.'s colleges generally seek those who plan to complete doctoral training as soon as possible. This pattern accounts to a considerable extent for the large proportion of "non-terminal" M.A.'s in academic positions. On the other hand, many of these non-terminal M.A.'s will in fact never complete their doctorates.

In practice, the terminal M.A.'s — those who do not plan further graduate training — often find employment of such a character that, strictly speaking, they cease to be members of the sociological profession. As is true with some of the jobs found by undergraduate majors in sociology, the training received is regarded as highly desirable by the employer, but the work context does not require or even strongly encourage the individual to retain and strengthen his identification with the discipline. Sibley shows that terminal M.A.'s are located in a very large number of quite different occupations.[3]

Both Tables 1 and 2 indicate that while roughly a quarter of the sociologists work outside the more usual kinds of academic setting, they are not heavily concentrated in any single field. Rather, they are thinly spread in various governmental fields, in certain areas of business, and in other private or semiprivate sectors of the job market. Between 1950 and 1959, at least, no very remarkable changes occurred in this picture. To give some notion of the diversity involved, there are terminal M.A.'s working in secondary education, in counselling, extension and administrative work in educational agencies, in nonacademic research of different kinds, in correctional agencies, in a variety of social work agencies, in religious denominations, in federal and state governmental agencies of several types, and in many large business firms, often in connection with personnel programs.[4] Ph.D.'s and non-terminal

[3] Sibley, *op. cit.*, pp. 57–59.
[4] *Ibid.*, pp. 57–59.

M.A.'s who are not academically employed often work for much the same kinds of employers as terminal M.A.'s. However, they are far more likely to be hired *as sociologists* whose specialized knowledge and research competence is what the employer wants.[5]

Demand and Supply in the Sociology Labor Market

The national character of the sociology labor market has certain quite important consequences, not least of which is the fact that the trained sociologist may seek employment almost anywhere in this country, in Canada, and to a lesser degree in other foreign countries, regardless of his present place of residence. The strongly academic character of sociological employment has a lot to do with producing this situation. Colleges and universities generally seek labor in nonlocal markets and sociology reflects this fact.

When it comes to describing the demand for sociologists we find, unfortunately, that no really adequate bookkeeping exists which collects such information in precisely relevant and periodic form. It is difficult to form estimates which can be regarded as highly reliable. Abbott L. Ferriss has prepared what is probably the best available review of both demand and supply factors in sociology.[6] Utilizing what information can be culled from direct and indirect sources, his article carefully and conservatively conveys about as much as can be said about this problem, and, where specific estimates are given, the present discussion relies heavily on his contribution.

At the present time and in the immediately foreseeable future at least, the largest demand for sociologists lies in the academic sector of the labor market. For decades sociology has been increasing in popularity with students, but the most significant factor at work now and for years to come is the dramatically

[5] An informative discussion of the employment of sociologists in the federal government can be found in N. Z. Medalia and W. S. Mason, "Position and Prospects of Sociologists in Federal Employment," *American Sociological Review*, 28, 1963, pp. 280–287.

[6] A. L. Ferriss, "Sociological Manpower," *American Sociological Review*, 29, 1964. The Department of Health, Education, and Welfare is preparing a systematic survey of demand and supply in sociology, but it has not been made available as yet.

rapid increase in college enrollments. Even with no increase in the proportion of students taking courses in the field, the growth in absolute numbers of students is already placing a very heavy strain on the supply of trained sociologists.

Ferriss estimates that, between 1961 and 1971, 3120 new full-time teachers of sociology will be required, a figure this writer now feels to be low.[7] Assuming that the proportion of persons holding doctorates when entering teaching remains the same as it is now, and taking into account an estimation of Ph.D. production during this decade, Ferriss comes to the conclusion that 1227 doctorates needed for teaching will not be available.[8] Very possibly, the shortage will be even greater.

What will happen in the academic portion of the labor market as a result of the shortage of fully trained sociologists? The general nature of the consequences is fairly clear. The proportion of sociology teachers holding the Ph.D. will decline for some years to come. Those with the degree will be even more heavily concentrated than at present in the universities with their graduate and research emphases. Four-year colleges will be unable to attract significant numbers of *new* Ph.D.'s to their faculties and will have to depend upon holders of the M.A. who will probably be available in reasonably adequate numbers.

While the nonacademic demand for sociologists has not shown rapid growth there are signs that this situation is changing. In a report to the President's Science Advisory Committee shortages of behavioral scientists are forecast as a result of many nonacademic sources of demand, particularly some of the new governmental programs.[9] Enough sociologists with the Ph.D. will not be available in the near future to satisfy nonacademic demand either. Some competition between collegiate and nonacademic employers for the services of sociologists can be forecast. In addition, the supply shortage will slow down the movement of soci-

[7] Ibid., p. 110. One reason for thinking these estimates low is the Vietnam conflict. More males are attending college and fewer dropping out as a result of the international situation.

[8] *Ibid.*, p. 110.

[9] The Behavioral Sciences Subpanel of the Life Sciences Panel, President's Science Advisory Committee, "Strengthening the Behavioral Sciences." Washington, D.C.: The White House, April 20, 1962.

ologists into nonacademic employment below what otherwise would take place simply because there will not be enough qualified persons to go round.

Another probable consequence of the supply-demand picture involves the M.A. "Terminal M.A.'s" are likely to be found in employment which is not centrally concerned with sociology and unlikely to be located in academic settings. It now seems likely that there will be an increase in the number of persons who intentionally complete their graduate training at the M.A. level and enter academic employment in four-year colleges, or take jobs as sociologists in government or industry. The jobs are there, and it is plausible to suppose that employers and job-hunting young sociologists will increasingly settle together on the assumption that the M.A. is terminal. This will mean an increase in the number of sociologists who have only the M.A. yet are firmly identified with the discipline and working within it.

CAREERS FOR WOMEN
IN SOCIOLOGY

In view of the shortages of sociologists likely to persist for years ahead it is worth while examining the possibility that women might help to fill the unmet need. Large numbers of women major in sociology as undergraduates. For many years more than half the undergraduate majors have been female.[10] Following the baccalaureate, however, there is a radical decline in the proportion of women who continue training in the discipline. In 1961–1962, for example, 73 per cent of the persons receiving the M.A. were male. For Ph.D.'s the proportion is even higher, about 85 per cent.[11] In short, while a great many women complete the first stage of sociological training, there is a great falling off in their numbers when it comes to the advanced preparation which leads to specifically sociological employment.

From the standpoint of the discipline's needs for additional personnel there is a regrettable wastage here. This situation is by no means confined to sociology, of course, and we know that since

[10] Ferriss, op. cit., p. 107.
[11] Ibid., p. 107.

1939 there has been a decline in the proportion of women on college faculties.[12] Strange to say, in an era in which the proportion of college-trained women has increased and women generally have been moving into the labor market in greater numbers there has not been an accompanying growth of feminine employment in the learned disciplines and professions, at least not as measured by academic employment. There is some scattered evidence that an increase of women moving into these fields may be forthcoming but it is far from convincing as yet.[13]

Fava cites a 1952 study on the proportion of women in sociology as compared with several fields:

> This survey shows that sociology occupies a middle-of-the-road position among the fields covered. Women made up 14.6 per cent of professionally employed sociologists, a proportion well below that in geography (18.4 per cent), linguistics and literature (21.8 per cent), anthropology and archeology (23.6 per cent), and art (29.6 per cent). On the other hand, the proportion in sociology was well above those in economics (6.1 per cent), political science (7.1 per cent), and philosophy (7.4 per cent). The proportions closest to sociology's were those in history and statistics (in each field, 12.7 per cent).[14]

Fava also reports that although salary differentials for males and females with comparable training and employment favor the male in sociology, they do so to a lesser extent than in a number of other disciplines, and also that relatively large numbers of women obtain the Ph.D. as compared with a good many other fields.[15] However, even after obtaining the doctorate in sociology women are more likely than men to drop out of active employment. If they continue in the labor market they are less likely than men to be active in professional affairs and to publish research.[16] On balance, then, women in sociology do quite well

[12] J. Bernard, *Academic Women*, University Park, Pennsylvania: Pennsylvania State University Press, 1964, p. 40.
[13] Bernard, p. 63.
[14] S. F. Fava, "The Status of Women in Professional Sociology," *American Sociological Review*, 25, 1960, pp. 273–74.
[15] *Ibid.*, pp. 272–276.
[16] N. Babchuk and A. P. Bates, "Professor or Producer: The Two Faces of Academic Man," *Social Forces*, 40, 1962, pp. 341–348.

when compared with women in other fields, but the really impressive fact is that there are so few demanding professional areas in which they play a major role.

A careful examination of the reasons lying behind this state of affairs would take the present analysis too far afield. It will be fairly obvious to most readers that there is some degree of discrimination against women in the professions and learned disciplines, including sociology, sad to say. In fields dominated by their sex men have not been notably generous in welcoming feminine colleagues. But it is equally evident that women themselves *have withheld* their participation. Jessie Bernard, who has published the best available analysis of women in the academic marketplace, considers both these factors in detail, then comes to this conclusion:

> Of the two images or myths or definitions of the situation — that the decline in proportion of women in academia is the result of a declining demand for their services, for whatever reason, or that it is a result of a declining supply of women offering their services — the second seems more nearly to conform to the facts.[17]

Women willing to undertake careers in sociology in the years ahead will find less difficulty in making their way. The new importance of the M.A. for teaching in four-year colleges will also help. Many women who are reluctant to seek the doctorate will find rewarding college teaching jobs if they have the M.A. In sum, providing only that more women are willing to enter graduate training and complete at least the M.A., it seems likely that there will be an increase in sociology's feminine contingent quite soon.

THE INCOME OF SOCIOLOGISTS

Most readers already know that one does not enter sociology to become rich. But since few Americans are attracted to careers requiring an ascetic renunciation of material values it is appropri-

[17] Bernard, *op. cit.*, p. 67.

ate to find out how well sociologists are financially rewarded for their services. Table 3 presents information collected by Sibley from his sample as of about 1962.

TABLE 3 • Median Annual Earnings of Ph.D.'s in Academic and Nonacademic Employment, by Age Groups*

	Academic Employment	Nonacademic Employment
All ages	$ 9,000	$12,000
Under 35 years	7,800	9,500
35 to 39	9,000	10,800
40 to 44	10,600	12,500
45 to 54	10,300	13,000
55 to 64	10,500	12,000

Sources: Schedules II, II-A (534 respondents).

* From E. Sibley, *The Education of Sociologists in the United States.* New York: Russell Sage Foundation, 1963, p. 53.

In interpreting these figures it is helpful to keep in mind that they apply *only* to the Ph.D.'s, and that the basic salary of college teachers, called the "academic year salary," is paid for services rendered during the nine-month academic year instead of the twelve-month year used in nonacademic employment. Academic people generally think of their salaries in terms of this nine-month period, although many also teach in summer sessions or are engaged in salaried research work during the summer months, or obtain additional income from consultative services. Although Sibley asked for "approximate annual earnings" it is not unlikely that the academic figures given are somewhat low. Still, as of 1962 at least, the chances are good that nonacademic employment paid somewhat better than academic.

More important, the figures are misleading because they do not adequately reflect the sharp upward direction of academic salaries in just the past few years. This is a direct result of the sudden spurt in college enrollments and the consequent alteration of the demand-supply ratio for college teachers generally, including sociologists.

Some indication of the changes taking place in a two-year period (1962–1963 to 1964–1965) is given in Table 4. Although this covers all disciplines it can be taken as broadly applicable to sociology.

Notice that the figures in Table 4 report nine-month salaries and that they show a distinct upward trend. The movement is virtually certain to continue for some years to come. Academic labor has for the first time in recent history entered a strongly competitive seller's market, and it may be taken for granted that most nonacademic employers of this kind of labor will be able to keep pace with the advance of salaries.

As this book goes to press academic demand is so sharp as to bring about at least temporarily a rather chaotic situation in salary competition. Schools of all types and qualities are bidding sharply with one another and the relative competitive situation of a given college or university can change quite markedly in the space of a single year. A sociology department may set out to employ assistant professors at, say, $8,000, and before the year is out be glad to fill their needs at $9,000. The fluidity of the market makes generalization difficult, but it is not far off to suggest that a young sociologist completing his doctorate in June, 1966, could readily find a good placement at academic-year salaries ranging between $8,500 and $10,000. In the same year a few high-ranking universities were paying some distinguished sociologists academic-year salaries in excess of $20,000.

College professors have not yet achieved the improvement of salaries relative to other highly trained professionals that they should, but the prospect is brighter than it has been in many years. There is increasing governmental and other societal recognition of the necessity for substantial improvement, and market forces are working powerfully in the right direction.

Another word should be said about supplemental income sources for professors. Probably the biggest source of income over and above the academic year salary is summer-session instruction. Enrollments in summer sessions have been increasing, more colleges are offering instruction in the summer, some institutions are

TABLE 4 · Comparison of Salary and Compensation Increases of Professors*

Weighted Average Salary and Average Compensation of Professors
in 1964–65 and Percentage Increases 1962–63 to 1964–65
by Type of Institution and Control [1]

(9-Month Basis, Institutions with Comparable Data)

	1964–65 Weighted Average		Dollar Increase 1962–63 to 1964–65		Percentage Increase[2] 1962–63 to 1964–65	
	Salary	Compensation	Salary	Compensation	Salary	Compensation
Universities						
Public	$13,054	$13,934	$1,464	$1,549	12.2%	12.5%
Private Independent	15,363	17,433	1,555	1,872	11.3	12.0
Church-Related	12,390	13,347	1,543	1,705	14.2	14.6
Liberal Arts Colleges						
Public	11,828	12,463	1,178	1,370	11.1	12.4
Private Independent	12,000	13,582	1,319	1,573	12.3	13.1
Church-Related	10,132	11,220	1,235	1,403	13.9	14.3
Teachers Colleges						
Public	11,045	11,328	1,279	1,327	13.1	13.5
Technical Institutions						
Public	12,215	12,528	1,494	1,571	13.9	14.3
Private Independent	13,549	15,245	1,538	1,785	12.8	13.3
Junior Colleges						
Public	11,338	11,886	839	1,145	8.0	10.7

[1] Numbers of professors in the current year were used as weights.

[2] Percentage increase is expressed as a per cent of weighted average salary (or compensation) in 1962–63.

* "The Economic Status of the Academic Profession: Taking Stock, 1964–65," AAUP Bulletin, 51, 1965, p. 256.

trying out the "trimester" system, and in general there is a movement toward year-round use of educational capacity. The end result is that a large and ever-growing proportion of college teaching staffs can find summer employment if it is desired. Stipends vary with the length of summer sessions and other factors, but summer teaching generally adds about two-ninths or 22 per cent of academic-year salary to a teacher's income. Thus, a college teacher whose academic-year salary was $12,000 and who taught in the summer session would have an annual income of $14,640.

A great many professors are decidedly ambivalent about teaching in the summer. The income may be welcome, but high-quality scholarship needs intervals of free time for study, reflection, and creative renewal. In universities, with their strong commitments to research, the recent availability of substantial public and private funds has made it much easier than formerly to finance summer research, including the professor's salary, and thus to have both the supplemental income and temporary freedom from teaching. This has led to a kind of tug-of-war involving the colleges' growing need for summer staff, the professors' desire to supplement academic year income, and their concomitant desire to have time for independent scholarly work during the summer (preferably with, but if necessary without, additional salary).

Some sociologists, although they are yet a small minority, also add to income by fees received for consultative services (usually involving their specialized research skills). As recognition of the sociologist's competence in many kinds of research useful to other specialists spreads this sort of arrangement will no doubt become more common. It will be intensified by the growing proportion of persons in the discipline who are well-trained researchers. Nobody expects to call on the skills of an engineer, architect, or attorney without paying for them, and the time is fast approaching when the sociologist's skills will be recognized in the market in the same manner. Too often in the past it has been assumed that the sociologist, unlike other professionals, offered his services free to anyone who asked.

At this point it should be clear that the outlook for employment in sociology is very good indeed. For years to come demand will exceed supply. Young people interested in the field occupationally need not fear that their services will be unwanted by society.

Training facilities are able to absorb more people than are now in training, and the financial rewards of work in the field are steadily rising.

It may have occurred to some readers that in absolute numbers the shortage of sociologists is not very great. As compared with many larger occupational fields this is true, but this does not make the shortages any less critical for those who wish to employ sociologists. The field cannot absorb a huge influx of new entrants in the next generation, but it will not be called upon to do so from either the demand or supply side. The real point is that sociology can offer careers to many more young Americans than have considered this possibility in the past.

THE WORK WORLDS
OF SOCIOLOGY

Having secured a quantitative picture of job opportunities in sociology it is time to look briefly *inside* the work worlds of sociologists. This brings to mind the distinction between an intellectual discipline and an occupation in which people make their livings. The first three chapters of this book are concerned with the first aspect; now we seek insight into the kinds of work done by sociologists as they earn their livelihoods by transmitting and enlarging the field of sociology.

It is not feasible here to survey the dozens of settings in which sociologists are employed. A more practical approach is to talk about the principal kinds of work done. At once the task is simplified, because there are just two kinds of work activity for which sociologists are by far most frequently employed: teaching and research. Each may be pursued in different settings, and, as we shall see, both may be performed by the same individual. Nearly three-quarters of all our sociologists are working in colleges and universities, so we begin with academic careers.

Teaching

The distinction between four-year colleges and universities is significant here. Many four-year colleges have separate departments of sociology. In others, sociology forms part of a division including a number of social sciences. The former arrangement usually implies a larger program of instruction in sociology, but majors in the field are frequently found in both settings.

Teaching undergraduates is the business of the four-year college. There is no graduate program and professors are seldom expected or encouraged to undertake research and writing. Teaching work loads vary, of course, but most range from nine to eighteen classroom contact hours per week. To the uninitiated this may not sound like much, but good teaching requires long hours of outside preparation. In addition, the professor is typically expected to make a good deal of his time available for individual consultation with students. The sociologist in the four-year college is engaged in general education. Very few of his students will be planning careers in sociology. As with all job settings, employment in a four-year college has both advantages and disadvantages for the sociologist considering career alternatives. Some specific factors can be listed, but it should be kept in mind that what is meat for one man is poison for another.

Above all, the four-year college is the place for the person who is strongly drawn to teaching young people, and this can be a magnificently rewarding experience. It is difficult, complex, often frustrating, but for the right person, full of intellectual challenge, excitement, and subtle rewards. In the four-year college the sociologist is free to make good teaching his dominant professional concern and his advancement will ordinarily be heavily based on assessments of his teaching effectiveness.

Both in and out of class the sociologist is likely to be better acquainted with his students than is possible in the university. He will know many of them as individuals and be more aware of how his work as a teacher impinges on the complexities of their young lives. His stake in what happens to them is consequently more personal than is generally true in the university setting. By the same token, more of his professional, even his personal life is visible and comprehensible to his students and he is perhaps more likely to serve as a model for them in various ways because they understand him better. In short, faculty and students are closer to each other in the four-year college than in the university. Their two worlds make contact and to a limited degree fuse more easily.

Academic departments in the four-year colleges are usually smaller than in the big universities, and this makes it easier for scholars in many disciplines to get to know one another and enjoy intellectual contact with other fields. Professors in large universities often move within tight disciplinary compartments with little interchange between fields. The entire academic community of the smaller school has a kind of compactness and relative ease of communication among its parts that many find extremely attractive. Another result of smaller size is that the institution is usually less bureaucratized, less burdened by complex impersonal procedures and paperwork.

These are some of the things that will appeal to persons who like the four-year college environment. However, the same persons may find some features not so much to their liking. Frequently, the comparatively heavy teaching load is spread across a wide variety of courses. The professor will not be equally well prepared or interested in all of them. The situation, on one hand, leaves little room for specialization and, on the other hand, requires an enormous amount of developmental work in order to do a good job in so many course areas. This may mean that the professor has little time for exploratory reading — "keeping up with the literature" as the phrase goes.

Some four-year college professors, while appreciating the opportunities to interact with men in other disciplines, may feel more cut off from others in their own fields than they like. Frequent contact with lively minds in one's own special area is one of the good ways to keep alert and to grow intellectually. Four-year college professors are what C. Wright Mills called "retailers" of knowledge.[18] In a sense they distribute knowledge to "consumers." If they also have impulses to become "producers" of knowledge the environment of the four-year college often discourages such impulses directly or indirectly.

In both four-year colleges and universities faculty members have two professional identities. They belong to the profession of college teaching, sharing this with teachers in all other disciplines and all institutions of higher learning. Simultaneously, they belong to the world of their disciplinary specialty, sharing this

[18] C. W. Mills, *White Collar*. New York: Oxford University Press, 1951, pp. 129–136.

locally only with other persons in the same field, but nationally with all other persons in that subject matter area. The profession of college teaching is represented by its own national organization, the American Association of University Professors. The A.A.U.P., as it is ordinarily called, is actively concerned with the welfare of college teaching as a whole in all institutions of higher learning, and keeps in touch with its membership through its journal, the *AAUP Bulletin.* On the other hand, each disciplinary field has its own professional organization furthering the interests of that field alone and not basically concerned with the problems of college teaching. Thus the two professional identities of the college professor are represented in his organizational affiliations.

In a small, four-year college which employs a single sociologist, say, a man has many local colleagues in the profession of college teaching but none at all in sociology. In the university this dualism of the professor's professional identity is more sharply drawn than in the four-year college, and involves greater potential conflict. In other ways, too, the university professor's work milieu has a more complicated structure. We shall examine the situation briefly.

Teaching loads are lower in the university, ranging from twelve hours of classroom contact per week downward. Senior staff members with heavy responsibilities for graduate supervision or research may teach as few as six or even three hours per week. The teaching load generally includes courses at both the undergraduate and graduate levels, the former often in large, impersonal classes, while the latter are typically small and involve more intimate contact with students. Close acquaintance with students and personal supervision of their work occurs mostly at the graduate level.

Graduate instruction and research account for lower teaching loads in universities. In sociology graduate programs, while the enrollment of graduate students is much smaller than that of undergraduates, supervision is extremely time-consuming, particularly in the area of thesis research. In most universities, faculty members are also expected to engage in creative work related to their discipline. The university professor, then, is expected to be a teacher of undergraduates, a teacher of graduate students, and a creative scholar. Small wonder that he often feels pulled now one way and now another, or unable to serve any of his tasks as well as he would like. Nor is it surprising, given these conditions, that university undergraduates often feel that their professors are not accessible to them.

Actually, the picture is more complicated still. The development of American universities into huge, complex organizations spending vast sums of money has produced elaborate administrative structures staffed with specialized nonteaching personnel. The professor lives in a world in which a great deal of power over decisions vital to him is located in "the administration." He must come to terms with this fact. In addition to his other duties, he must participate in the committee structure and other administrative affairs of his department, of his college, and of the university as a whole. He may regret the time needed for this, but is likely to feel that the faculty must retain its contact with "the administration" if the latter is to function effectively in serving the academic goals of the university.

To say that his work brings him into contact with undergraduate students, graduate students, the administration, his discipline (local and national), and the profession of college teaching still doesn't do justice to the situation. The point is that, while related, these are to a surprising extent separate and quasi-autonomous social worlds. Each has its own traditions, folkways, values, and internal structure. The world of the graduate student is different from that of the undergraduate. The world of the administration of the university is different in significant ways from that of the profession of college teaching, and both are different from the many disciplinary worlds which are locally manifest in the dozens of departments of the university. All these worlds are of course interdependent; they share the same home, but in the vastness of today's big universities they have grown considerably apart and communication between them is far from perfect.

The college professor is the one person in the university who at least is in direct contact with all of these social universes. He alone has at least a slight personal acquaintance in them all. On the other hand, the persons he meets in one sector may have only a vague idea of his commitments and obligations in the others, since they know him directly in only one of his professional roles. With each part of the academic community making demands on him it really is not possible for even the most conscientious professor to do a first-class job in *all* areas, and the need to allocate scarce time and energy to so many tasks is one of the most difficult problems of the university faculty member.

A word or two should be said about the notorious phrase "publish or perish." It refers, of course, to the demand that the university scholar must do creative work in his own discipline, typically resulting in some form of scholarly publication. It is true that the professor's advancement is more likely to depend upon his professional creativity than on *any other single factor*. But the phrase "publish or perish" has come to imply that professors typically produce shoddy work, anything at all so long as it gets into print, in order to win promotions or pay increases.

Some scholars do turn out trivial work, and a much larger number feel the external pressure on them to "produce." But the meaning currently given to the phrase is misleading and unfair. It overlooks the fact that a large proportion of university scholars do research and publish their findings because they are deeply interested in their subjects. The encouragement to engage in pioneering at the frontiers of knowledge is one of the factors that attracted them to the university. And the easily cynical interpretation so often encountered also overlooks the fact that the productive labors of university scholars are essential to the whole organized process by which human knowledge is advanced in our society.

Despite the problems found in academic careers, on balance, college teaching must surely be one of the most attractive occupations available today. Higher education is entering the most exciting period in its history. The great winds of change sweeping through society are blowing through the campuses too. Institutions of higher learning are hard-pressed at a dozen points. They are far from perfect. They struggle daily with problems which seem sometimes to be insuperable, but they are alive and vital. And they are far from being mere recipients of changes originating elsewhere in society. Because they are absolutely essential to the maintenance and enlargement of society's pool of knowledge and talent in a dynamic age they also have a profound effect upon the future. The old ivory tower image really must be discarded once and for all. Academic careers should not appeal to those who want soft and easy jobs. Because the challenges are great and complex much is demanded of those who link their personal futures with today's colleges and universities.

Research

The word "research" is nowadays so commonplace and so loosely used that its meaning is ambiguous. Here it refers to a kind of activity that is, literally, indispensable in all scientific disciplines. Although in everyday speech people speak of "researching" something — meaning only that information is to be sought — this discussion refers to processes that intellectually and procedurally are a good deal more rigorous than popular usages customarily imply.

Not all sociologists do research, but the advancement of the field manifestly depends upon those who do. It is one of the major work worlds of sociology. The specific settings in which research may be done are too numerous to discuss in detail here. The pages above have made it clear that creative research is a normal expectation for university sociologists who may be located in departments of sociology (where some teaching is expected). It is also customarily expected of sociologists in professional schools (where teaching may or may not be involved), and in campus-based research institutes of various kinds. On the other hand, the research sociologist may be found in many noncampus locations too, such as commercial polling or market research firms, in many agencies of the federal government and some more local governmental units, in private agencies concerned with social problems of one kind or another, in private, nonprofit research groups, and others. In many of these places the sociologist will spend all his time in research. While we cannot do justice to this diversity, there is enough similarity about the conduct of sociological research, wherever located, so that it can be described in general terms which convey at least something of the reality.

Planning Research • To begin with, how does a sociologist choose a problem for research? The answer may involve a host of factors. Outside an academic sociology department the choice will be affected by the special interests of the employer. If the sociologist works in a medical school, for instance, his research will certainly have some kind of relevance for the medical profession. In any setting, of course, the scholar has developed more interest in some parts of sociology than others.

Perhaps, though, for nonsociological reasons, a scholar is just more interested in some kinds of problems than others. He may feel that greater professional rewards will accrue from working in one area rather than another. Or, he may feel much better qualified to do one kind of research than another. His choice of a problem may reflect the comparative importance it is seen as having in the discipline at the time (and these emphases change, often in quite illogical ways). He may choose to work in a particular area because he can get financial support there with relative ease, or he may have strategic access to an exciting research setting. His choice may reflect an attitude that research should have practical as well as theoretical justification; or he may hold just the opposite view.

It may seem odd, but one of the most difficult stages in research is this first one where it is necessary to set forth a problem which is clear in its objectives, worth doing from the standpoint of its contribution to knowledge, and feasible within the available research technology and resources the scholar may tap. A variety of factors ultimately point the researcher in one among innumerable possible directions. Then putting his ideas into sound and workable shape for the task is a taxing and disciplined kind of work.

It is necessary, for instance, to become fully conversant with previous work bearing directly and often only indirectly on his project. Previous work includes both theoretical and empirical research materials. To what extent is there agreement or disagreement in these materials, and what are the implications for what he intends to do? He will want to avoid the pitfalls encountered by his predecessors. Again, he may be seeking to clarify or resolve an important conflict in earlier evidence. Are there detectable logical or methodological errors in existing work, or perhaps clues to variables which others overlooked and he may include in his analysis?

All this search and reflection on the "literature" is important because of the *accumulative* character of scientific knowledge. Our sociologist proposes to add a few more pieces of information to the common stock, but he wants to fit them into an organized and growing structure, not toss them onto a disorderly unrelated heap of facts. Unless he does this, much of his painstaking work is wasted. Furthermore, this operation (often supplemented by professional shoptalk with colleagues) may lead him to make revisions in his original idea.

While still in the early stages of planning the researcher must undertake to locate whatever financial support is needed. Many modest projects may require no dollar outlay, while at the other extreme, the sociologist may have in mind a massive research program extending over several years and costing hundreds of thousands of dollars.

Sooner or later, and regardless of where he is employed, the researcher is likely to become acquainted with the complexities of fund-seeking. The government agencies and private foundations which are the sources of most money for sociological research have detailed formal procedures for fund applications. The researcher is scarcely given a blank check. He must describe his plans, justify the worth of his ideas, indicate in some detail how the money will be spent, and submit all this information in the many duplicate copies beloved by all bureaucratic organizations. Sometimes he may anticipate a "site visit," in which representatives of the granting agency come to his place of work to survey the feasibility of his plans at close range.

As he looks ahead the researcher tries to lay out an orderly progression of events, and subsequently will struggle to maintain it in the face of all the unforeseen contingencies which await him. He will try to think through his theoretical ideas as fully as possible in advance, specifying, for instance, the hypotheses to be tested and the kinds of evidence he will need to test them. Moving outward from the research problem itself, he will confront and make decisions on a great multitude of matters involved in implementing his ideas. Are there existing data-gathering methods he can employ or modify, or must he invent new ones? What specific techniques of data analysis will be most appropriate to his problem? If he plans to sample from a larger population, what sampling method will be most feasible and satisfactory? What assistants will he need — how many and of what kinds of specialized competence? How will they be housed and supervised? Is the necessary data processing equipment available? These few illustrative questions convey the fact that a large project may involve the researcher in very substantial logistic problems.

A short description of some of the working tools of the research sociologist will help at this point to envisage his task.

Collecting and Analyzing Information • Very likely, many laymen fondly imagine that they have some understanding of the research techniques used by natural scientists. Although the conviction is mostly illusory it is come by naturally enough. After all, the "hardware" of the physical scientists has been given constant and glamorous exposure in the mass media. This is not true of the methods most frequently used by social scientists, and furthermore, they do not possess to the layman's eye the same massive (and somehow thereby convincing) physical presence. But the sociologist does have his own growing stock of research tools for collecting usable data and subjecting information to careful analysis. Most are shared by his fellow scholars in other social sciences rather than being his exclusive property.

One important group of techniques may be described as "observational," because the investigator is in a position to collect his information while the behavior being studied is actually going on. Small group sociologists, for example, have devised methods for classifying the content and quantitatively recording the frequency of interaction in studies of groups. In laboratory group settings it is possible to closely approximate the conditions of controlled experimentation. Some methods must be used only by specially trained observers, and no deliberate cooperation from research subjects is required.

Another, less controlled form of observation is called "participant observation." This refers to a situation in which the investigator becomes part of the natural social setting which is his object of study. However, unlike other members, he retains a detached perspective, from which he carefully notes and makes records of the behavior in which he is interested. An especially well-known study using this technique is one by William Whyte in which Whyte lived for several years among the street-corner gangs of young, unmarried men in an ethnic slum of Chicago.[19] On other occasions the sociologist may simply arrange to be present at a social event (perhaps a riot, crowd, or audience) in which he is professionally interested. He remains outside the situation, so to speak, but closely observes what goes on.

Interviewing continues as a basic research technique in sociology. The degree to which it is structured varies widely. In some instances, particularly at the beginning of a research program, the investigator starts out with only a few broad questions and encourages the respondent to range freely about the subject matter, with probing questions interjected occasionally. Here the researcher is usually feeling his way, unwilling to decide as yet what more fixed form his main investigation will take.

Starting with this kind of interviewing, there are many degrees of increasing specificity as to the form questions (and answers) may take. Finally, there is the situation in which all questions are carefully worked out in advance, asked in just the same way of all respondents, and answers are possible only in predetermined categories. This kind of instrument is usually called a "schedule." In this form, data are easily subjected to statistical analysis, a procedure which is much more difficult with the less structured forms of interviews. Even in the "looser" interviews, though, it is possible to codify answers in forms permitting quantitative analysis, by application of methods called "content analysis."

Questionnaires are similar to schedules, but as we use the term here they are self-administered. The respondent may fill them out in a large group setting where someone is usually present to give instructions and to pass out the instruments and collect them. Or, the questionnaire may be sent through the mail. Again, questions are highly specific and answers must fall into categories furnished on the instrument.

[19] W. F. Whyte, *Street Corner Society*. Chicago: University of Chicago Press, 1943.

People are so accustomed these days to schedules and questionnaires of one kind or another, and to the casual eye they appear so simple in construction, that it would seem anyone could devise such a tool. Sociologists often find their students eager to do a piece of research using a schedule or questionnaire thrown together in an hour or two. Often, too, there are requests to fill out such instruments where it is evident to the trained eye that an amateur hand is at work. The deceptive simplicity and the ready adaptability of these tools to a vast array of nonscientific goals sometimes chagrins sociologists and other social scientists.

The truth is that the construction of worthwhile schedules and questionnaires is a demanding, subtle task, with pitfalls abounding. A complex technology for their construction has grown up among social scientists to whom they are such important adjuncts to research. A typical specimen takes a great deal of skilled work to construct, and usually undergoes careful "pre-testing" to reveal flaws before the final form is established. Often the investigator has concealed in his instrument groups of questions which will be used to construct *indices* representing some phenomenon, or *scales* intended to measure degrees to which a measured variable is present. Such indices and scales are tested by standard techniques to ascertain whether or not they are *valid*, i.e., measure the things they are supposed to measure, and *reliable*, i.e., can be counted on to produce the same kinds of results from one time to another.

Under the name "public opinion polling" the use of short, rigidly designed schedules with carefully drawn samples has become perhaps the most widely recognized research technique of the behavioral sciences. The familiar polls reported in the press are commercial enterprises and their primary goal is not the production of scientific information, although the best ones have won respect in scientific as well as nonscientific circles. Their proprietors are usually conversant with and make use of the research technology associated with scientific studies. For scholars, among whom this body of techniques is even more highly developed, the term "survey research" identifies an increasingly sophisticated research technology.

For survey research and many other kinds of research in sociology a matter of utmost importance is sampling. For many reasons it is often not feasible to contact all the members of a large population, and the investigator must be content with interviewing a small proportion of the total. This at once raises a serious problem because the smaller proportion (sample) should be representative of the entire population. This means that if the questions asked of the sample were put to the entire population the distribution of answers would be the same in both cases. If this condition cannot be met (or approximated within known levels of confidence) there is no way of knowing whether or not the findings of a study hold good for more than the sample studied. Once again, a complex technology of sampling methods has developed which allows researchers to solve this kind of problem with considerable confidence.

In this short list of research techniques the use of documentary materials should be included, since it is one of the oldest of them all and is still widely used, particularly in combination with other methods. The previous examples are cases in which a sociologist goes out and collects his own original data for the special purposes of his study. With documentary sources he uses material already in existence which often has a public character and availability. For instance, the information collected by the U.S. Bureau of the Census is a fundamental source of data for sociologists, as it is for so many others. So are the official statistics of many other federal, state, and local agencies. Documents of many other kinds may be used, such as newspaper records, moving picture scripts, and magazine contents.

Once information has been gathered by one or a combination of means it must be subjected to analysis which will set forth its significance for hypotheses being tested. A wide variety of methods is available. By and large, whatever method is chosen, the goal in a large proportion of cases is an essentially *quantitative* statement about the relationships between the factors and variables being studied. It is rather rare to find instances of research in which the *sole* objective is to give a purely descriptive account of a single social phenomenon. For this reason the techniques used to express relationships quantitatively in sociology are increasingly statistical in character. At this point in the history of the field it is hardly possible to be a research sociologist without some competence in methods of statistical analysis, and training in this area is a standard part of graduate work.

Like so many other specialists, sociologists are rapidly adapting to the enormously increased efficiency of modern computers, which enable them to undertake quantitative research of a size and complexity entirely beyond the discipline's resources until very recently. The computer's possibilities for information storage and retrieval will also play an increasing role in the work of the research sociologist.

Final Stages of Research · When all the evidence has been collected and applied to testing the hypotheses with which a researcher began, important steps still remain. Did the data lend support to the hypotheses? If so, the research scholar never maintains that the hypotheses were *proven*. After all, he has only tested them one or a few times in one or a few of many possible sets of circumstances. Nevertheless, support for the hypotheses will be seen as adding confidence to the basic theoretical assumptions or postulates from which the hypotheses themselves are derived.

Perhaps the empirical facts failed to support the hypotheses or did so only partially or in an ambiguous way. The researcher must ponder the import of such outcomes. Did his research design fail to provide an adequate test of the hypotheses? Were the results attributable to imperfections in the information gathered? Or (having considered these possibilities), does the situation appear to call for a reappraisal of the theoretical framework underlying the entire research? It is the researcher's responsibility not only to report what he found but to evaluate its significance in such ways as these.

The next task is to report the research in a form accessible to other interested scholars. Ordinarily this means that articles will be submitted to the editors of professional journals, or books or monographs will be written and publication will be sought through one of the commercial or university presses. Since the pressure of scholarly work upon publication outlets is heavy there is no guarantee that the research will make its way into the body of scholarly literature. But if it is of high quality the chances for such exposure remain good. And it is important that this be so, since all that has gone before will be lost if the new research findings cannot take their place in the larger context of knowledge to which they are related.

Very often, too, the researcher must make a final report to the agency supplying funds for his work: this may have been a condition of the grant in the first place. Also, the reported success of the scholar in carrying out his plans may affect his chances of securing support for the next research project he wishes to undertake.

Consultation

While a large majority of the duties performed by sociologists can be classified as some form of teaching or research, the growing importance of the consultative services they render should also be mentioned. Like the other two, this kind of work may be done in a wide variety of circumstances. Underlying all the variations is a relationship between a sociologist and a "client." The sociologist is approached by a potential client who wishes to enlist his aid in securing ends of his own. Either he feels that the sociologist's knowledge of human behavior will be helpful to him or he desires expert assistance in a research program in which the skills of the sociologist are appropriate, or both.

The client may be an organization, a business firm, a government agency, a civic or welfare organization, or may be an individual, possibly a researcher in another discipline, or another sociologist. The relationship may be brief, confined to a single or a few sessions in which the sociologist analyzes the client's situation and offers advice. On the other hand, it may be extensive in time if warranted by the circumstances. The client pays the sociologist a consulting fee much as is done in other professions where similar relationships occur. Consulting work generally occurs outside the sociologist's usual job obligations. Relatively few have become full-time consultants. However, the rapid growth of the consultant's role in the field may lead to a noticeable increase in the number of persons making their livings this way.

The sociologist, wherever located, is a man or woman whose

vocation has both problems and great opportunities. His youthful discipline is undergoing extremely rapid and uneven evolution. It takes strenous effort to keep abreast of even those sectors of the field most important to him and to relate his own work to the constant flow of new ideas and research findings. As a teacher he participates in all the problems of keeping higher education viable in a society which itself is changing at breakneck speed. As a researcher he is pressed by the need to keep abreast of new research techniques and findings and to see clearly how his own work relates meaningfully to the development of the field's basic knowledge of human behavior. He is also importuned by outsiders for assistance and counsel, and experiences difficulties in developing his own thinking and research efforts along the line he wishes while at the same time lending professional assistance to outsiders with *their* problems.

All the same, it is an exciting period for sociology and the sociologist. A democratic society is awakening to the possibilities of the behavioral sciences, and the demand for their services is steadily increasing. The society is tolerant enough and wealthy enough to give sociologists and other behavioral scientists the freedom and support they need in order to do first-rate scientific work. In the middle of the twentieth century sociology has an opportunity to grow vigorously and demonstrates its ultimate usefulness to man. At this moment, too, a "help wanted" sign hangs on the discipline's door. More young people are needed who would like intellectually adventurous careers in sociology as it faces up to the challenges and opportunities afforded it in the generation ahead.

VII

SOME CRITICISMS AND PROSPECTS

More than once in this book we have alluded to the fact that sociology is a comparatively young discipline which is not as yet very well known to the general public. Many people have only extremely vague ideas of what the word "sociology" denotes. Among those familiar with the word, if not the field, one sometimes encounters criticisms which are a result of misinformation, occasionally associated with a feeling that sociology is threatening to valued interests. In discussing this subject we hope to avoid suggesting a certain paranoid attitude attributable to a youthful field of knowledge. Every area of scholarship is and must remain open to relevant criticism. Still, sociologists would prefer to be taken to task for what sociology is rather than for something it is not.

In the intellectual world particularly one finds a stereotypical image of sociology.[1] While the edges of the image are somewhat indefinite and the whole picture varies from one setting to another, here are some of its more familiar components. The sociologist may be seen as committed to a collectivist ideology, as a cold manipulator of men, a clumsy, superficial do-gooder fascinated by the pathological in behavior, a scholar producing trivial

[1] A very good discussion of this whole subject can be found in B. M. Berger, "Sociology and the Intellectuals: An Analysis of a Stereotype," *Antioch Review*, 17, 1957, pp. 275–290.

or obvious findings, one who is concerned with subjects which are better treated by other specialists, a person who is insensitive to the nuances of human experience, and the possessor of a barbaric jargon which is used to write unreadable prose!

Assembled in one place and put so bluntly, these facets of the stereotype portray a horrendous fellow indeed! The picture is not usually encountered in this form, however. Typically, such notions are isolated in brief, oblique references in novels, poetry, literary criticism, drama, the press, and conversation among intellectuals. Examples are so numerous that any well-read person will encounter many. A quite characteristic illustration is found in the first sentence of a review of a novel titled *491*, by Lars Görling. "There is probably not a sociological treatise in print with the insight and impact of Lars Görling's fictional case '491' — or a novel with such blatant sociological intentions." [2] Without pausing to comment on this sample of the genre let us briefly examine the elements of the image listed above.

Sociologists sometimes run across the notion that they hold social organization to be more important and valuable than the single person, an idea which is far from the truth. Social behavior is the *subject matter* of the field; sociologists are people interested in this subject matter. To deduce their social philosophies from their subject matter is no more warranted than to predict how a man personally feels about the latest Supreme Court decision if all we know about him is that he is an attorney.

A contradictory quality appears in the idea that sociologists are impersonal or ruthless manipulators of people and at the same time ineffectual do-gooders. Since we are speaking of what is probably a number of overlapping but not identical stereotypes, and since stereotypes are not developed logically, this is not so surprising. The reader of this book will not need to be told that neither of these ideas is descriptive of sociology or of the typical professionals within it. The source of the "cold manipulator" component may be the sociologist's use of statistical techniques in research. These indeed are impersonal, but of course this in no way implies that the sociologist uses such devices to control the lives of people.

[2] Review in *Newsweek*, August 1, 1966, p. 87.

The do-gooder idea may well stem from the popular confusion of sociology and social work about which comment was made in an earlier chapter. Why is it so often assumed that the subject matter of sociology deals exclusively with the seamier sides of society? Perhaps the *fact* that the field has studied what most would call social problems for many decades is the source, although it is simultaneously true that there has been continuous interest in behavior that would be regarded as normal. Of course, pathological behavior is more attention-getting, and since many know the sociologist studies it, *ergo*, that must be the whole subject matter of the field.

There is no more persistent misconception about sociology than the conviction that "everybody already knows" the things that sociologists discuss. Closely related, if less commonly met, is the idea that the sociologist brings a ponderous and unwieldy scholarship to bear upon trivial problems.

The "everybody already knows" charge is not brought against, say, physics and chemistry, although every living human being unfailingly obeys the laws revealed by these sciences. The difference is that people *subjectively* experience the subject matter of sociology in categories of perception not too radically different from those used by the sociologist. Culture furnishes ready-made interpretations of this experience and there appears nothing more to add. Chapter I discussed the special qualities of the sociological perspective which, applied to everyday experience, reveal not only the inadequacies (for some purposes) of common-sense, "everyone knows" interpretations, but also the great mysteries that reside in the commonplace.

On the subject of triviality it may simply be pointed out that, by lay standards, many problems studied by sociologists are in fact of the greatest consequence. Yet it is true that, judged by these same lay standards, some problems might appear to be trivial, since — rightly or wrongly — sociologists are interested not only in the peaks and valleys of social life but also in the plains where everyday life jogs along placidly enough most of the time. *All* social experience is the sociologist's province.

Another contradiction appears in the comparison between the criticism just mentioned and the complaint that the subjects treated by sociologists are done more justice by other scholars. Since other scholars are sometimes the sources of both indictments this might be seen as concession that the work of other specialists dealing with the same subject is also trivial! But logical consistency is not to be expected here.

Although sociology has a unique point of view to contribute to the understanding of human behavior, *when this point of view is not grasped* the field may appear to be preempting the roles of older disciplines. For example, the literary artist and the historian have been immersed in the portrayal of human behavior for a vastly longer period than sociology. Because the sociologist is a newcomer it may be easier for him than for those in literature and history (and several other areas) to understand that both ends and means differ among these fields, so they are not really competitors at all.

It is no more appropriate for a sociologist to judge a poem or a novel by the standards of his discipline than it is for a poet or novelist to find that a sociological treatise fails to meet the standards of his craft. Consider literature. To those who love it, literature is indispensable. Among other things it sharpens our awareness of being alive, expresses and intensifies our feelings, gives aesthetic form and meaning to experience, and reconciles us to the human condition. What could be more important than such functions as these? We wish only to note that they are different from the functions of sociology and the other behavioral sciences, and in this stage of civilization the latter too are important. Science's way to a form of truth is not the way of art or of religion, but it does relate significantly to the deep human desire to understand, and it does add measurably to the tools available to man for coping with his problems, old and new.

Chapter I made it clear that the sociological perspective concentrates on the social rather the purely individual aspects of behavior. This task specialization does not mean that sociologists argue that the social level is important and the individual level of behavior insignificant. We say this since it is true that the sociologist is not professionally sensitive to aspects of the individual which are unique to one person alone, and sometimes it is precisely these that other scholars feel are most crucial.

The same point should really be made again for social psychology since so many sociologists also work in that field. Here, it might seem, the idiosyncratic in individual behavior should be taken into account. Not so, however. Once again, the social psychologist (even though the individual may be a unit in his analysis) is striving to produce empirically supported theories about human behavior. These are probability statements applying to all individuals or to those in designated categories. He is not trying to communicate to a reader the full richness of individual variation. But it is not accurate to assume from this that nonprofessionally he is any less sensitive to "nuances" than anyone else.

Finally, there is the matter of sociological jargon. The sociologist is charged with being peculiarly adept at clumsy neologisms, at forced re-definitions of familiar words, in general, at creating an opaque vocabulary accessible only to the initiated. What is overlooked here is that *all* scientific fields must construct symbol systems characterized by the maximum attainable accuracy and precision. More broadly speaking still, all extensive groupings based on long-term interests develop "jargon" terms which carry specialized meanings for insiders. The "humanistic" critics of sociology's professional language are not exceptions to the generalization.

Sociology's difficulty here is due in part to the fact that it has so often incorporated words from everyday speech into its vocabulary. When it does so it deliberately strips away from the words the delicate connotations and ambiguities which constitute their richness in another context, but which are unacceptable in scientific analysis. To do so may seem an affront when the purpose is not understood.

As we leave this subject, it should be conceded that every one of the criticisms noted, not to mention others, can be supported here and there in the work of sociologists. There is sociological research and writing that is obvious or trivial or jargon-ridden and all the rest. At the same time, there is sociological work that is penetrating, important, and even gracefully written (though elegance in style is not an *objective* of sociology). Unfortunately, there are poor sociologists as well as good ones, just as there are both third-rate and first-rate novelists, poets, historians, and journalists. Most people would rather have their occupations and professions judged by the best work produced, not the poorest.

A FINAL WORD:
SOCIOLOGY'S PROSPECTS

Today sociology is out of its swaddling clothes and no longer an infant. Both as a field of knowledge and as a body of professionals it has achieved a sense of identity, of continuity, and of confidence. There is an internal momentum to the field and a sufficiently established place in society to insure its future. Although some criticisms of sociology have just been discussed, more significant is the fact that increasing acceptance and even understanding of its nature and potential are met on almost every hand.

While sociology, and the other social sciences, are of course not intensely interesting to everyone, it is possible to argue that some exposure to their evolving perspectives and knowledge is now essential for the education of anyone who wants a reasonably adequate understanding of the kind of world inhabited by twentieth-century man. Sociology is growing at a phenomenal if somewhat uneven rate, both as a field of knowledge and as an occupation. It is in the former sense, naturally, that the import of its growth is greatest for society. The total number of *sociologists* will always be relatively small, but the impact of *sociology* will loom increasingly large.

It is already a significant part of the general education programs of millions of young Americans in college. If the past is any clue to the future, this contribution will expand with the passage of time. Simultaneously, a different kind of relationship to society will become evident in the growing use of sociological knowledge by policy-makers in every major sector of activity. Sociology (and almost as crucial, the awareness and recognition of sociology) have progressed to the point at which the discipline's knowledge and its professionals will be taken into account in practical affairs to a degree quite unknown in the past.

Many problems will attend this development. We believe that most sociologists will probably wish to have a primarily consultative role in public or private decision-making, but there will be counterpressures to handle. Sociologists and their clients still have a great deal to learn in working out mutually acceptable relationships. Meanwhile, society will furnish in increasing amounts the support for research the field must have if it is to grow as a basic scholarly and scientific discipline.

The reader must not suppose that we are heralding some triumphant dawn in which the sociologist will suddenly emerge as the wise leader of men and solver of all man's ancient and modern social ills. He, at least, has no such fantasies. In the first place, he knows that the level of his knowledge makes such a role impractical and the character of his discipline inclines him to avoid it firmly. Second, although his point of departure in studying man is different, he knows as well as any Freudian psychoanalyst the degree to which man is inherently irrational and emotional as well as a creature of reason and restraint. Both in his goals and the means chosen for attaining them man cannot be expected to be coldly rational and scientific, and the sociologist knows it. Despite all this, where man should or can use intelligence and knowledge in the conduct of life, sociology becomes an increasingly valuable servant at his disposal.

In the meantime there is much work to do, and working conditions are better than they have ever been before. Sociology needs able young recruits today, and there is time to enter a field still in its exciting early history. If it is getting late to be like one of the mountain men who first penetrated and explored the Old West, there still is time to be one of the pioneers who, after the mountain men, cleared the wilderness, settled it, and turned it to useful purposes.

In this short book it has been possible only to introduce a number of topics pertaining to sociology as a discipline and a profession. We hope that some readers will be tempted to learn more. The readings listed below are carefully chosen to permit an interested person to probe more deeply into many different aspects of the field, and to do so without having to undertake an extensive bibliographic search in an unfamiliar field. The chapters of this book for which each work is especially appropriate are indicated at the right.

For Chapter

B. Berelson and G. A. Steiner, *Human Behavior, An Inventory of Scientific Findings.* New York: Harcourt, Brace & World, 1964. An ambitious attempt to summarize the findings of research in all the behavioral sciences.   2, 3

P. L. Berger, *Invitation to Sociology.* New York: Doubleday & Co., 1963. A lively, informal presentation of the field for lay readers. Well written.   1, 2, 3, 7

L. L. Bernard and J. Bernard, *Origins of American Sociology.* New York: Thomas Y. Crowell, 1943. An important reference on the history of the field.   1, 4

W. B. Cameron, *Informal Sociology*, Studies in Sociology. New York: Random House, 1963. A diverse and entertaining collection of essays on matters sociological.   1, 2, 3, 7

R. E. L. Faris (ed.), *Handbook of Modern Sociology.* Chicago: Rand McNally, 1964. An important set of articles covering much of the field, written primarily to the professional.   1, 2, 3

For Chapter

A. W. Gouldner and S. M. Miller (eds.), *Applied Sociology, Opportunities and Problems*. New York: Free Press, 1965. The title aptly identifies the thought-provoking and illuminating contents.　　　　3

P. E. Hammond (ed.), *Sociologists at Work*. New York: Basic Books, 1964. Fascinating discussions of the research process by experienced sociologists discussing their own work.　　　　3, 6

R. C. Hinkle, Jr. and G. J. Hinkle, *The Development of Modern Sociology*, Short Studies in Sociology. New York: Random House, 1954. A good short history and characterization of sociology which does not extend into the most recent years.　　　1, 2, 3, 4

A. Inkeles, *What Is Sociology?*, Foundations of American Sociology Series. Englewood Cliffs, N.J.: Prentice-Hall, 1964. A short and authoritative introduction to the fundamentals of sociological knowledge.　　　　1, 2, 3

R. K. Merton, *Social Theory and Social Structure*, rev. ed. Glencoe: Free Press, 1957. Chapters 2 and 3 are particularly recommended for the clarity with which the relationships between theory and research are presented.　　　　3, 6

R. K. Merton, L. Broom, and L. S. Cottrell, Jr. (eds.), *Sociology Today, Problems and Prospects*. New York: Basic Books, 1959. Somewhat uneven in quality, these papers (prepared for an annual meeting of the American Sociological Association) nevertheless constitute an important resume.　　　　2, 3

E. Sibley, *The Education of Sociologists in the United States*. New York: Russell Sage Foundation,

For Chapter

1963. A significant milestone in the development of sociology as a profession. Rather specialized for the nonprofessional reader.   5

G. Simpson, *Man in Society*, Studies in Sociology, New York: Random House, 1954. Interesting short accounts of sociology, several other social sciences, and the relations among them.   2, 3

R. Thomlinson, *Sociological Concepts and Research*. New York: Random House, 1965. A good introduction to the field, with special emphasis on research methods.   1, 2, 3, 5, 6

D. M. Valdes and D. G. Dean, *Sociology in Use*. New York: Macmillan, 1965. Presents a wide variety of settings in which sociological knowledge has been found to have practical value.   3

E. K. Wilson, *Sociology, Rules, Roles and Relationships*, Homewood, Ill.: Dorsey Press, 1966. For those readers who have not encountered an introductory text with its extensive coverage of sociological content, this stands high on the list of good ones.   1, 2, 3

1965 Guide to Graduate Departments of Sociology. Washington, D.C.: American Sociological Association, 1965. Useful information for the student thinking of entering graduate training.   5

The American Sociologist, published quarterly by the American Sociological Association. All issues contain matters of interest to the professional sociologist.   4, 5, 6